Navigating Adversity

2nd Edition

A Self-Care Field Guide for the Mission Critical Mind

Dr. Renee Thornton & Rodger Ruge

Cover design: David Ter-Avanesyan/Ter33Design LLC

Library of Congress Cataloging-in-Publication Data

Names: Thornton, Renee, author. | Ruge, Rodger, author.

Description: Fennville, MI: Pathfinder Resilience Publishing, 2021 | Revised and updated edition of Navigating Adversity: Tactical Self-Care for First Responders, originally published in 2021 | Includes biographical references and source citations.

Summary: In an applicant pool of one hundred, only four meet the psychological standards for mission-critical work. You are the 4%: wired to protect, selected to serve, equipped for what others can't handle. But no one taught you how to protect the very psychological makeup that uniquely qualifies you for this work. Navigating Adversity is the research-validated toolkit for building wellness across every dimension: physical, psychological, cognitive, emotional, spiritual, financial, social, and professional. Used by more than 10k mission-critical professionals, this second edition delivers what most wellness programs miss—including the critical distinction between true burnout and the understimulation that mimics it. There is no resilience without adversity. You were built for both. Now build the capital to sustain it.

Our goal is to provide books for high performers who challenge the status quo. We hope you enjoy the read!

Every resource in this book and the associated practicum was intentionally built for those who serve others first.

To Chesney for insisting that I stop letting fear stand in the way of publishing my work.
~ Dr. Renee Thornton

To Colonel James "Jim" Fraser for the relentless push that forced me to confront the writer inside.
~ Rodger Ruge

Contents

FOREWORD

Chief (ret.) Joseph Fox, NYPD 1981-2018

Serving as a public safety professional is the best job in the world. There's nothing like being the first one in and the last one out of a critical incident and knowing that you and your team saved lives. The dream for all of us who wear the uniform is that we'll leave our cities safer than we found them. Doing that demands of us an attitude of self-care that few of us realize is at the very center of our success.

We push hard, give much, and focus our efforts on everyone…except us. That is, until we're so depleted that words like burnout, compassion fatigue, and despair become part of our mental vocabularies. For many of us, this happens long before we've even hit the peak of our careers, and for far too long we've learned to live with the negative impact of the adversities we face. Not because we want to live life feeling depleted, but because we never took the time to learn how to refuel.

At a time when most wellness resources are focused on preparing for that one big critical incident, Navigating Adversity reminds us of one very simple truth: the highest quality of service to others reflects the care we give ourselves. Put simply, if we are well, we will do well by others.

Doing well starts with a proper understanding of what wellness is. For many, it is simply the strength, flexibility, and nutritional demands of the physical body. In recent years, mental and emotional considerations have been added to the definition. However, a thorough understanding cannot stop there. It must also include the boundary-pressing truth that we are all spiritual creatures with a sense of duty driving our purpose, that our financial choices are impacted by our social fit and professional growth, and ultimately that the attitudes we take determine how we see ourselves and the world around us.

Every day we make choices that impact just how healthy we are. Even in my busiest times, I have acknowledged the need for me to be well but that doesn't mean I always was. There are moments I look back on and see clearly how distracted I was. Sometimes I welcomed the distraction because looking too closely was painful. Other times, I didn't even notice the distraction until I felt myself nearing depletion. Like a trauma you don't see coming, some of our coping choices result in long-term health complications that we can't see until they arrive as high blood pressure, alcoholism, obesity, and diabetes. For many of us, we live unconsciously incompetent. We don't know what we don't know about ourselves. But we can change that.

Navigating Adversity is a tactical self-care field guide that walks you through all eight dimensions of wellness, with a focus on what you can do to effect change in your own life. The job is difficult, sure, but it's what we signed up for. We can't let ourselves fall apart and then blame the uniform or the department or the things we've seen. We are either as healthy or unhealthy as we choose to be. Take time for yourself.

As you work your way through this book, listen to what your body, mind, and spirit are telling you that they need. Honestly evaluate your decisions and the impact they have on your wallet, your tribe, and your career. At the conclusion of your experience, you will have a new appreciation for how unique you truly are and be inspired once again to live a daily life of purpose, passion, and fulfillment.

Chapter One

There Is No Resilience Without Adversity

> *Within the core of each of us is the child we once were. This child constitutes the foundation of what we have become, who we are, and what we will be.*
>
> **– Neuroscientist Dr. R. Joseph**

Somewhere right now, a young person is sitting in front of a hiring panel, palms sweating, trying to articulate why they want this job. They've rehearsed their answers, studied the department, maybe even driven past the station a dozen times imagining themselves walking through those doors.

They're talking about wanting to make a difference, to serve the community, to be part of something bigger than themselves. And every word is true. What they don't know – what no one tells them – is that the very qualities making them perfect for this job are the same qualities that will make it so hard to survive it intact.

If that young person is you, or if it was you years ago, this book is written specifically for you.

The Four Percent

You have chosen one of the most honorable professions in existence. The enthusiasm you felt the day you were hired – that sense of purpose and possibility – is evidence that you were once the picture of hope, optimism, and self-confidence. For many, the decision to become a first responder stems from childhood adversity, whether personally experienced or witnessed in others. This means you likely started this work with a certain amount of resilience already built into your character.

Here's something most people don't know: in an applicant pool of one hundred, only about four candidates on average meet the psychological and emotional standards required to succeed in this profession. You are part of the four percent. You were screened and chosen for specific characteristics – traits that qualified you for work that most people couldn't handle.

The problem? No one told you what those characteristics were.

Without that awareness, it becomes almost impossible to notice when time and exposure to human dysfunction and trauma start eroding the very qualities that made you exceptional in the first place. The optimism fades so gradually that you don't realize it's gone until you catch yourself wondering when you became so cynical. The confidence gets chipped away call by call until you're not sure you trust your own judgment anymore.

A Note for Those Wired Differently

You may have noticed something about yourself over the years: under intense pressure, while others scramble for coping techniques, something in you just *activates*. You don't consciously decide to stay calm – you just do. You don't think through your decision-making process – you assess and act.

Research identifies 10 psychological skills that predict success in mission-critical work – skills present in roughly 4% of the population. You likely possess most or all of them. And here's what matters for this book: these skills are your *default response* under pressure. They're not techniques you deploy. They're how you're wired.

But here's what the research also shows: these skills are perishable. Not because you'll forget to use them – you won't – but because the default itself can weaken. The emotional regulation that was once automatic can become effortful. The judgment that was instinctive can start requiring conscious thought.

This book exists to help you maintain what makes you exceptional. Not by teaching you skills you already possess, but by giving you the tools to keep those skills sharp – so your default response remains strong when you need it most.

FIELD PERSPECTIVE

"I remember my first year on the job – I was going to change everything. By year five, I just wanted to survive my shift. By year ten, I didn't recognize the person I'd become. Nobody warned me that the job could do that. Nobody told me there was another way."

– Patrol Officer, 16 years of service

The Conversation Nobody Has

Think back to the day you were chosen for your first position. Now imagine that before heading off to training, you sat down with your new supervisor and heard something like this:

Welcome to the team! We're genuinely excited to have you on board. Soon you'll be sent off to training, which is going to focus on the mechanics of this job – the skills, the procedures, the knowledge you need to do the work safely and effectively.

Here's what they won't teach you: how to keep your hope, positivity, and inspiration alive throughout your career. Hard days are coming. Days that will challenge everything you believe about yourself, about people, about whether any of this matters. And when those days come, the culture will tell you to suck it up, push through, and not let anyone see you struggling.

We're telling you now: that approach will destroy you. Not might – will. So, here's what we want you to understand from day one: taking care of yourself isn't weakness. It's the only way to have a career instead of a countdown to collapse.

If you'd heard those words, would you still have taken the job? Probably – which is exactly why you belong in this field. But imagine how different your career might look if someone had equipped you with that understanding from the beginning.

That's what this book is designed to do.

Understanding Your Why

Replenishing what you give to others is known as self-care, and it speaks directly to your personal why. Why did you decide to dedicate your life to the service of others? Why is this job important to you? The answers to these questions reveal what inspires you to serve – but they say even more about what you believe.

If your answers have anything to do with wanting to change the world, make it safer, help people, or protect the innocent, then you carry within you something precious: idealism. As an idealist, you possess both a gift and a responsibility. The optimism that idealists feel is what drives change in the world.

Without it, humanity would simply accept things as they are and deteriorate. Optimism is a core belief that things can be better and that you have the power to make a difference.

This book begins with a simple premise: you deserve to be happy. You deserve to live a long, healthy life filled with success and meaning. You can and should become stronger, better, kinder, and more impactful. No matter what adversity you've already survived, you can overcome its setbacks. No matter what adversity awaits you, you can prepare yourself in advance and reduce its impact.

All you need are the right tools and a little direction.

Moving Beyond the Deficit Model

Traditionally, the adverse consequences of stress and trauma have been treated using what's called a deficit model. Experiencing flashbacks? You must have post-traumatic stress disorder. Not sleeping? A sleep disorder. Feeling panicked? Panic disorder. The deficit model looks at what's wrong with a person and assigns a diagnosis.

There are significant problems with this approach, especially for first responders:

- It assumes there's something abnormal about flashbacks, sleep disturbances, and other responses to traumatic experiences – when in fact, these are often normal reactions to abnormal situations.

- A disorder diagnosis can further traumatize someone who's already frightened about what's happening to them and who fears professional consequences for seeking help.

- It requires people to wait until their symptoms meet a specific clinical threshold before they can receive professional support – by which point, the damage may be severe.

There are certainly times when diagnosis is necessary. When symptoms are so acute that medication is needed to provide relief while underlying causes are addressed. When a mental health crisis is so severe that immediate intervention is required to save a life. But even with a clinical diagnosis, with rare exceptions, full recovery is possible. With the right tools, education, and support, human beings have an extraordinary capacity to heal and grow from pain.

The Shift To 'Injury' Language

Throughout this book, you'll notice we primarily use the term Post-Traumatic Stress Injury (PTSI) rather than Post-Traumatic Stress Disorder (PTSD). This is intentional.

The word 'disorder' implies something is fundamentally wrong with you – a permanent condition that defines you. The word 'injury' acknowledges that something happened to you that caused damage, and like any injury, it can heal with proper care.

This isn't just semantics. Language shapes how we think about ourselves and our struggles. An injury is something you recover from. A disorder is something you manage forever. We believe the injury framework is more accurate, more hopeful, and more conducive to healing.

Why First Responders Don't Seek Help

Research consistently identifies four primary reasons first responders avoid mental health treatment. These findings have remained remarkably stable over the past decade – the same barriers that existed when this work began in 2010 persist today:

1. Concerns about confidentiality – fear that seeking help will become known to supervisors, peers, or the department
2. Failure to recognize symptoms – not understanding that what they're experiencing has a name and a solution
3. Doubt that providers understand – skepticism that a therapist could possibly grasp the unique challenges of the profession
4. Fear of peer judgment – worry about colleagues' discovery and subsequent loss of faith in their abilities on the job

As you'll soon learn, these are the exact same fears that kept Rodger Ruge, one of the authors of this book, from asking for the help he needed to cope with the traumas this job exposed him to. His story, shared in the chapters ahead, demonstrates both the cost of suffering in silence and the possibility of complete recovery.

The Landscape Is Changing

When this work began, California's passage of SB 542 – recognizing PTSI as a presumptive illness for first responders – was groundbreaking. It was one of the first legislative acknowledgments that the psychological wounds of this profession deserved the same recognition as physical injuries.

The landscape has shifted dramatically since then. A 2024 review found that 28 states now cover first responder mental health claims under Workers' Compensation statutes, with additional states having implemented non-Workers' Comp policies for mental health support. The federal Helping Emergency Responders Overcome (HERO) Act directed the CDC to create a

Public Safety Officer Suicide Reporting System, bringing unprecedented attention to the mental health crisis in our profession.

These policy changes matter. They signal that society is beginning to recognize what we've known for years: the psychological demands of first response work are real, the consequences of ignoring them are devastating, and support systems must be built into the profession rather than bolted on as an afterthought.

But policy alone won't save you. The tools in this book will...but you must use them.

FIELD PERSPECTIVE

"I finally went to a therapist after my third divorce. She specialized in first responders – understood the job, the culture, the things we see. That made all the difference. I wish I'd gone fifteen years earlier. I'd still have my first marriage."

– Fire Captain, 24 years of service

The Reality of Exposure

Half of all adults will experience or witness a traumatic event during their lifetime. First responders, by contrast, are exposed to an average of three critical, traumatizing incidents for every six months they serve. Add to that the chronic stress of the job itself – organizational dysfunction, public scrutiny, physical demands, irregular schedules – and the cumulative load becomes staggering.

But here's what's important to understand: for many first responders, the trauma that causes deterioration doesn't stem from a single catastrophic incident. It's not necessarily the worst call that breaks you. More often, it's the relentlessness – the repetitive exposure to human suffering, the organizational betrayals, the expectation that you'll witness something shocking and then continue your shift without processing what happened.

This matters because it means you don't need to wait for a "bad enough" experience to justify taking care of yourself. The daily grind counts. The accumulated weight of ordinary calls counts. The political dysfunction in your department counts. When treated as a reality for which intervention doesn't exist, it takes a toll. When treated as something that can be prepared for in advance, positive outcomes are within your control.

The Institutional Betrayal Factor

Recent research points to something that many in the mission-critical field have known intuitively for years: organizational betrayal can be more damaging than external trauma.

Betrayal trauma occurs when harm is perpetrated by someone you have a close relationship with or a high degree of trust in – a supervisor who throws you under the bus, a department that fails to support you, a system that prioritizes liability over your wellbeing. This kind of abuse of trust often causes more lasting damage than trauma perpetrated by strangers.

Studies show that institutional betrayal is associated with higher rates of PTSI, depression, anxiety, and substance abuse than equivalent trauma from external sources. It creates internal conflict and doubt about purpose, calling, and faith in institutions that should represent the best society has to offer.

If you've experienced this kind of betrayal, know that your reaction isn't weakness or oversensitivity. The research validates what you feel. And the tools in this book can help you heal from it.

Trauma Affects Different People Differently

An essential truth about self-care is understanding that trauma impacts different people in different ways. Two officers can respond to the same fatal accident – one processes it and moves on: the other carries it for years. Neither response is right or wrong. Both are human.

The factors that determine impact are complex: your personal history, your support systems, your current stress load, your genetic makeup, even what else happened that day. Some people can witness a mangled body and see only a scene to be processed. Others become overwhelmed by the sights, sounds, and smells, and the incident leaves a wound that must either be properly treated or left to fester.

Because scenes of human suffering affect different people differently, it's essential to become your own expert. No one else can tell you what should or shouldn't bother you. Your reactions are your data – information about what you need, not evidence of what's wrong with you.

The Bank Account Metaphor

Rabbi Cary Friedman offers a powerful way to understand your wellness: think of it as a bank account.

When you entered this profession, you were likely filled with energy – physically fit, determined, hopeful about the future. Your confidence was high, both in your own abilities and in the importance of the work. Think of that as starting your career with an overflowing account – ten billion dollars on day one.

Every interaction, every experience, either deposits into or withdraws from that account. Positive, fulfilling encounters add capital. Negative encounters – giving of yourself to someone else, having something taken from you – withdraw it. The degree to which an exchange impacts you determines the size of the transaction.

Understanding your personal withdrawal and deposit patterns is crucial. Dr. Gary Chapman's work on love languages provides one framework: if your primary language is words of affirmation, a supervisor's public commendation creates a massive deposit; public criticism causes a devastating withdrawal. If your language is acts of service, different exchanges will carry different weight.

The deeper insight is this: you cannot rely solely on others to make deposits. The goal of this book is to teach you how to build your own capital – how to replenish your accounts regardless of whether your environment is supportive or toxic, whether your calls are good or bad, whether life cooperates or fights you every step of the way.

Defining Wellness

Surprisingly few comprehensive definitions of wellness exist in the research literature. Physical health focuses on bodily function. Behavioral health emphasizes coping mechanisms and choices. Psychological definitions lean toward cognitive and emotional aptitude – and unfortunately, are often framed in deficit terms like mental illness and emotional instability.

One of the most powerful lessons from working with first responders on this project is that wellness is multidimensional. You cannot be truly well while neglecting any major dimension of your life.

When this work began, we focused on mental, emotional, spiritual, and physical health. Over time – through countless conversations and feedback from first responders across the country – we've expanded our definition to include social wellness, professional development, and financial health. We've refined our approach to mental health to encompass both cognitive processes and the psychological attitudes expressed by world-class performers: Olympians, military service members, physicians, entrepreneurs, and the most resilient first responders.

The result is our working definition: Wellness is the intentional pursuit of self-care through the accumulation and expression of spiritual, cognitive, emotional, physical, social, professional, financial, and psychological capital.

Each of these dimensions will be explored in the chapters ahead, paired with the specific adversities that threaten them and the practical tools for building capital in each area.

The Common Adversities

Decades of research have identified specific mental health challenges that first responders face when they don't practice regular self-care. These challenges rarely appear in isolation – more commonly, they arrive in pairs or clusters, each reinforcing the others:

- Occupational stress – the chronic, cumulative burden of the job itself
- Post-Traumatic Stress Injury (PTSI) – the wound left by acute or repeated trauma exposure
- Depression – the loss of hope, energy, and engagement with life

- Anxiety – the persistent state of worry, dread, or panic
- Addiction – the reliance on substances or behaviors to cope
- Compassion fatigue – the depletion that comes from caring for others without replenishing yourself
- Institutional trauma – the damage done by organizational betrayal and toxic work environments

In the chapters that follow, each of these adversities is addressed in detail and paired with the capital type most effective at countering it. You'll learn not just what these challenges look like, but what to do about them – and equally important, how to distinguish between true clinical conditions and organizational conditions that mimic them.

When It Looks Like Depression but Isn't

The adversities listed above are real. Depression, anxiety, PTSI – these are clinical conditions that require appropriate treatment. But emerging research reveals something crucial that the deficit model consistently misses: not everything that looks like depression *is* depression.

Consider the officer who presents with low energy, loss of interest, and emotional flatness. The deficit model sees depression. But research from the *Journal of Neuropsychiatry and Clinical Neurosciences* distinguishes between depression – which involves emotional pain and hopelessness – and apathy, which involves feeling nothing at all. Depression responds to certain treatments. Apathy may worsen with those same treatments.

Or consider the firefighter who seems checked out, irritable, and going through the motions. Is this burnout from overwork, or boredom from underwork? A 2024 study in *Scientific Reports* confirmed that boredom is "not simply a milder form of depression, but represents a distinct state and trait disposition" that requires different interventions entirely.

This matters because you – the four percent – are not wired like the general population. Research on sensation-seeking shows that people drawn to high-stakes professions have neurobiological differences in how they process stimulation. The APA has noted that "high sensation-seeking is a normal personality trait" that "plays a role in bringing people into prosocial occupations such as law enforcement, firefighting, and emergency room medicine."

When your work stops providing the challenge your neurobiology requires, you may experience something that *looks* like depression but is understimulation. The treatment implications are opposite: rest and reduced workload – the standard prescription – may remove what little stimulation remained and accelerate your decline.

This book focuses primarily on building capital across all dimensions of wellness. But as you work through the chapters ahead, keep this question in mind: *Is what I'm experiencing a mental health condition requiring clinical intervention, or is it an organizational condition requiring environmental change?*

The answer determines whether the tools in this book are sufficient, or whether you also need to examine the fit between who you are and where you work.

Know Yourself, Know Your Enemy

In The Art of War, Sun Tzu wrote:

If you know the enemy and know yourself, you need not fear the result of a hundred battles. If you know yourself but not the enemy, for every victory gained you will also suffer a defeat. If you know neither the enemy nor yourself, you will succumb in every battle.

Running into danger, being surrounded by evil, and regular exposure to human suffering is a battle you have chosen to fight. Doing it well demands more than mechanical mastery of your job. It requires that you pay keen attention to the signals your body and mind send you – recognizing the early warning signs of adversity before they become crises.

Once you know what you're facing, you can use the tools in each dimension of wellness to intentionally refuel what you've spent in service to your community. That's what resilience is: not the absence of struggle, but the capacity to recover and grow from it.

There is no resilience without adversity. And there is no adversity you cannot overcome with the right preparation, the right tools, and the commitment to your own wellbeing

Chapter One Reflection

Take a few minutes to consider the following questions. There are no right answers – only honest ones.

- What drew you to this profession in the first place?
- How has your relationship to that original motivation changed over time?
- Which of the four barriers to seeking help resonates most with you? Why?
- If you imagine your wellness as a bank account, what's your current balance?
- What are your primary wellness withdrawal sources right now?
- What are your primary wellness deposit sources – and are they reliable?

Chapter Two

The Physical Systems and Our Impact on Their Wellness

Adversity: Occupational Stress & Environmental Assault

It's 0300 and you're four hours into what's already been a brutal shift. The call volume has been relentless, and somewhere between the domestic disturbance and the overdose, you realized you never ate dinner. Now you're parked in a fast-food drive-through, engine idling, staring at a menu of options that all lead to the same place: temporary satisfaction followed by the familiar fog of regret.

You know better. You've heard the lectures, seen the statistics, maybe even watched a colleague's health collapse under the weight of years of neglect. But right now, at this hour, with cortisol still coursing through your system from that last call, knowing better feels completely irrelevant. You just need something – anything – to fill the emptiness and get you through to end of watch.

This chapter is about understanding what's happening inside your body during moments like these, and why the choices that feel easiest in the short term are often the most expensive in the long run. But more importantly, it's about giving you practical tools to make different choices – not through willpower alone, but through understanding

> **FIELD PERSPECTIVE**
>
> *"I spent fifteen years eating my way through night shifts, telling myself I'd get healthy 'after this case' or 'when things slow down.' Things never slowed down. My wake-up call came at 47 when I collapsed in the locker room with chest pains. I'm still here, but I lost five years to recovery that I could have spent with my kids."*
>
> **– Retired Sergeant, 22 years of service**

Understanding Your Body's Alarm Systems

When your body detects stress – whether it's a call to a violent scene or a tense conversation with your supervisor – it activates what we might think of as three different alarm systems. Each one is designed to help you respond to danger, and together, they're the reason you can perform under pressure when others freeze.

Adrenaline is your instant-response siren. It hits your system within seconds of a perceived threat, spiking your heart rate, sharpening your focus, and flooding your muscles with energy. It's why time seems to slow down during a critical incident – your brain is processing information at an accelerated rate.

Norepinephrine is your focus-sharpening signal. Working alongside adrenaline, it heightens your alertness and concentration, helping you zero in on what matters while filtering out distractions. It's what allows you to hear a suspect's whispered command over the chaos of a crowded scene.

Cortisol is your sustained-alert system. Unlike adrenaline's rapid spike, cortisol builds more slowly and stays in your system longer. It's meant to keep you functional during extended periods of stress – raising your blood sugar, suppressing non-essential functions, and keeping your body in a state of readiness.

These systems work beautifully for short-term crises. The problem is that your profession keeps these alarms ringing long after the immediate threat has passed. And cortisol, in particular, was never designed to run continuously. When it does, it starts causing damage.

The Cortisol Problem

Chronic cortisol elevation leads to:

- Fat storage around the midsection (even with exercise)
- Elevated blood sugar and insulin resistance
- Suppressed immune function
- Disrupted sleep architecture
- Impaired memory and cognitive function
- Increased inflammation throughout the body

Eustress vs. Distress

In your training, you were likely taught to use your body's stress response to your benefit. In short bursts, stress enhances performance – this is called eustress, or beneficial stress. It's what you feel before a foot pursuit or when you're problem-solving a complex investigation. Your body rises to meet the challenge, and you perform at levels that would be impossible in a relaxed state.

But there's a threshold. When stress becomes chronic – the result of prolonged exposure to difficult calls, organizational dysfunction, and the constant low-grade vigilance your profession demands – it transforms from fuel into poison. Acute stress from a single traumatic event and chronic stress from cumulative exposure both lead to the same destination: premature aging, disease, and diminished capacity to do the job you love.

The most common manifestations include gastrointestinal issues, unexplained weight gain (particularly around the midsection), acid reflux, cardiovascular problems, elevated blood pressure and cholesterol, and diabetes. The mental health consequences are equally severe: depression, anxiety, and the increased likelihood of turning to substances to cope.

There's another threshold that rarely gets discussed: the point at which stress becomes insufficient. Research on person-environment fit reveals that your body responds to underload – work that fails to match your capacity for challenge – with many of the same physiological markers as overload. For the four percent, a job that has become routine, bureaucratic, or stripped of meaningful challenge can trigger cortisol elevation, sleep disruption, and systemic inflammation just as surely as trauma exposure. If you're experiencing physical symptoms despite what looks like a "manageable" workload, consider whether the problem might be too little meaningful demand rather than too much.

> *In order to change, people need to become aware of their sensations and the way that their bodies interact with the world around them. Physical self-awareness is the first step in releasing the tyranny of the past.*
>
> **– Bessel A. van der Kolk, MD,**
> **The Body Keeps the Score**

Your Body as Early Warning System

Your body is constantly communicating with you. When you entered this profession, you came into it knowing there would be days when your body would be pushed to its limit and others when sitting for hours would be required. What you may not have known is that your body is not only your instrument for action – it's your early warning system for everything from minor physical issues to major mental and emotional distress.

Unfortunately, most of us were never taught to interpret the body's signals. We learned to push through discomfort, to ignore fatigue, to override the messages our systems were sending because the mission came first. This capacity for endurance is part of what makes you effective at your job. But it's also what makes first responders so vulnerable to catastrophic health failures that seem to come out of nowhere.

The goal of this chapter is twofold: first, to remind you of the physical systems you rely on for health and to help you recognize the warning signs of distress in each. Second – and this is where this edition differs significantly from the first – to reveal the hidden threats that are silently undermining your health in ways you may never have considered.

The Hidden Health Threats

When we talk about public safety, mission-critical health, the conversation usually centers on the obvious culprits: stress, trauma, shift work, and the physical demands of the job. These are real and significant. But there's an entire category of health threats that rarely makes it into wellness training – threats that are accumulating in your body right now, quietly setting the stage for chronic disease.

We're talking about what researchers call "body burden": the cumulative load of environmental toxins, endocrine disruptors, and inflammatory agents that your body is processing every single day. And here's the uncomfortable truth: many of the convenience solutions that help you survive the demands of your job are accelerating this burden.

What's Really in Our Food

Let's start with the most immediate challenge: what you're eating. The time poverty inherent in your profession – irregular hours, unpredictable call volume, limited break windows – creates a perfect storm for poor nutritional choices. You don't have time to prepare meals. You eat when you can, where you can, and speed usually trumps quality.

But here's what's happening behind the scenes of that fast-food meal or grocery store convenience item:

Grocery store meats from conventional sources are routinely treated with antibiotics, growth hormones, and various additives. These don't just disappear when you cook the meat – they enter your system and accumulate. Growth hormones in particular can disrupt your own hormonal balance, contributing to weight gain, mood disturbances, and metabolic dysfunction.

Processed foods are engineered – literally designed by food scientists – to override your body's satiety signals. They're formulated to hit the precise combination of salt, sugar, and fat that triggers maximum dopamine release, creating a neurological response similar to addiction. That's not hyperbole; it's documented food science. The same companies spend billions ensuring that their products are, in the industry's own language, "craveable."

Hidden ingredients lurk behind vague label terms like "natural flavors" and "artificial colors." These can include MSG (which triggers hunger), preservatives linked to inflammation, and dyes that some research connects to behavioral issues and cellular damage. The average processed food contains ingredients that didn't exist in the human diet a century ago.

The DoorDash Dilemma: Paying Premium Prices for Chronic Disease

Food delivery services have become a lifeline for exhausted first responders. After a brutal shift, the idea of cooking feels impossible. A few taps on your phone, and hot food appears at your door. It's convenient. It's easy. And it's quietly destroying your health and your finances.

Let's do the math that nobody wants to do:

- Average food delivery order: $25-35 (including fees and tip)
- If you order delivery just 3 times per week: $75-105 weekly
- That's $3,900-5,460 annually – on food that's making you sick

But the real cost isn't financial. Restaurant food – especially the kind that travels well and shows up at your door – is designed to taste good, not to nourish you. Portions are larger than necessary. Sodium content is often triple what you'd use cooking at home. Ingredients are selected for cost and shelf stability, not nutritional value. And the convenience of not having to think about food means you're outsourcing one of the most important decisions you make each day to corporations whose only incentive is your repeat business.

Here's the uncomfortable reality: every time you tap that delivery app, you're paying a premium price to have chronic disease delivered to your doorstep. The convenience isn't free – you're financing it with years off your life and quality of life in the years you have left.

FIELD PERSPECTIVE

"I tracked my spending for one month and realized I was dropping over $600 on delivery and fast food. That's a car payment. I started meal prepping on my days off – nothing fancy, just proteins and vegetables I actually like – and I'm saving $400 a month while feeling better than I have in years."

– Dispatcher, 8 years of service

Endocrine Disruption: The Invisible Assault

Your endocrine system is like a sophisticated internal messaging network. Hormones serve as chemical messengers, carrying instructions throughout your body telling systems when to activate, calm down, grow, or repair. This network controls everything from your metabolism and mood to your sleep patterns and stress response.

Endocrine disruptors are chemical compounds that hijack this communication system. They mimic your natural hormones, block real hormones from doing their jobs, or scramble the messages entirely. The result? Your body's internal communication breaks down, leading to a cascade of problems: unexplained weight gain, persistent fatigue, mood swings, reduced immune function, fertility issues, and increased cancer risk.

What makes endocrine disruptors particularly insidious is that they're everywhere – and most people have no idea they're being exposed.

In Your Water

Bottled water seems like a healthy choice – and compared to sugary drinks, it is. But those plastic bottles leach microplastics and chemical compounds into the water they contain, especially when they're exposed to heat (like sitting in your cruiser on a summer day) or stored for extended periods. Recent studies have found hundreds of thousands of microplastic particles in a single bottle of water. These particles don't just pass through your system – they accumulate in your tissues and organs.

Tap water brings its own concerns. Depending on your municipality, it may contain elevated levels of heavy metals (lead, copper, arsenic), chlorine byproducts, pharmaceutical residue from improperly disposed medications, and agricultural runoff including pesticides and fertilizers. The "safe levels" established by regulatory agencies are based on individual contaminants – not the cumulative effect of dozens of compounds interacting in your body.

Solution: Water Filtration

Invest in a quality water filtration system. We recommend ProOne, Epic Outdoorsman, Aquasana, or the Zero Water pitcher and filter system. Each is known for removing a variety of dissolved solids, heavy metals, and contaminants. Using water filtration systems is an affordable initial investment with reasonable ongoing filter costs, and it's portable – you can filter water at home and bring it with you in glass or stainless-steel containers.

The bottom line: Ditch single-use plastic bottles entirely. Your water shouldn't be poisoning you.

In Your Body Products

Every morning, you probably use shampoo, soap, deodorant, and lotion without a second thought. But flip those bottles over and look at the ingredient lists. What you'll find are chemicals that would require a chemistry degree to pronounce – and many of them are known endocrine disruptors.

Parabens (methylparaben, propylparaben, butylparaben) are preservatives used in cosmetics and personal care products. They mimic estrogen in the body and have been found in breast cancer tumors.

Phthalates are used to make fragrances last longer and plastics more flexible. They've been linked to hormone disruption, reduced sperm count, and developmental issues.

Synthetic fragrances are perhaps the most concerning because of a regulatory loophole: companies can list "fragrance" as a single ingredient while hiding dozens of individual chemicals behind that term. Many of these hidden chemicals are known endocrine disruptors, allergens, and neurotoxins.

Your skin is your largest organ, and it's remarkably absorbent. What you put on your skin goes into your bloodstream – often faster than if you'd swallowed it, because topical absorption bypasses the digestive system's filtering mechanisms. Every product you use is a delivery system for whatever's in it.

In Your Home

The assault doesn't stop when you leave the bathroom. The products you use to clean your home, wash your clothes, and make your living space smell pleasant are often loaded with the same problematic chemicals.

Laundry detergent and fabric softener are particularly concerning because whatever's in them stays on your clothes – against your skin – all day. And if you're wearing a uniform for a 12-hour shift, that's half your life spent in contact with these chemicals. Synthetic fragrances in laundry products don't wash out; they're designed to bond to fabric and release slowly.

Dryer sheets coat your clothes in a thin film of synthetic compounds. That "fresh" smell? It's a cocktail of chemicals including benzyl acetate (linked to pancreatic cancer), benzyl alcohol (a respiratory irritant), and chloroform (a neurotoxin). Every piece of clothing that goes through a dryer with sheets comes out covered in this residue.

Air fresheners and plug-ins are continuously releasing synthetic fragrances and volatile organic compounds into the air you breathe. A 2006 study found that air fresheners emit an average of 18 different chemicals – and many products failed to list the majority of these on their labels.

The Accumulation Problem

Here's what makes this particularly concerning for first responders: these exposures don't happen in isolation. You're drinking water from plastic bottles in your cruiser, wearing a uniform washed in chemical-laden detergent, applying products loaded with synthetic ingredients, and grabbing food that's been processed, preserved, and packaged.

Each individual exposure might be 'within safe limits' – but those limits were never calculated for the cumulative load you're carrying. And when you add occupational stress (which suppresses immune function and impairs your body's detoxification pathways) to this chemical burden, the effects compound.

Practical Solutions: Taking Back Control

Reading all of this can feel overwhelming. You might be thinking: "Great, one more thing I have to worry about. As if I don't have enough going on." We get it. But here's the reframe: these are factors you can control. Unlike the trauma you'll witness on duty or the dysfunction in your department, your food choices, your water source, and the products you allow into your home are entirely within your power to change.

And unlike many wellness recommendations that require massive lifestyle overhauls, these changes can be incremental. Start with one. Build from there.

Food: Returning to Source

The fundamental principle is simple: eat food that your great-grandparents would recognize as food. If it comes in a package with ingredients you can't pronounce, it's not food – it's a food-like product engineered for profit, not for your health.

Building relationships with local food sources transforms eating from a mindless convenience into an intentional act of self-care:

- Farmers markets connect you directly with the people who grow your food. You can ask questions, learn about growing practices, and know exactly where your food comes from.
- Community Supported Agriculture (CSA) programs deliver fresh, seasonal produce directly to you. Many offer payment plans and first responder discounts.
- Local ranchers and farmers can provide meat without hormones, antibiotics, or mystery additives. Buying in bulk (half a cow or pig) often costs less per pound than grocery store prices.
- Growing even a few things yourself – herbs on a windowsill, tomatoes on a patio – reconnects you to what real food is.

As for the time challenge: batch cooking is your answer. One focused session of 2-3 hours on a day off can produce a week's worth of meals. Store them in glass containers (not plastic), and you have grab-and-go nutrition that's genuinely nourishing. Compare the cost and time of that one prep session to a week of delivery orders, and the math becomes obvious.

Body Products: The Switch

You don't need to become a chemist or make everything from scratch (though some find that satisfying). The simplest starting point is subtraction: eliminate the most problematic products and replace them with cleaner alternatives.

- Start with the products you use most: deodorant, soap, shampoo. Switch to unscented versions or products with ingredient lists you can read.
- Castile soap (like Dr. Bronner's) is a versatile, simple-ingredient option that works as body wash, hand soap, and even household cleaner.
- Coconut oil-based deodorants, while different from antiperspirants, eliminate the aluminum and synthetic fragrances found in conventional products.
- A general rule: if you can't pronounce it, question whether it belongs on your body.

Home Environment

- Switch to fragrance-free laundry detergent. Your clothes don't need to smell like a chemical approximation of 'mountain spring.'
- Replace dryer sheets with wool dryer balls. They work just as well for static and softening, without coating your clothes in chemicals.
- Remove plug-in air fresheners. If you want your home to smell pleasant, open windows, use an essential oil diffuser with pure oils, or simmer cinnamon and citrus on the stove.
- When cleaning products run out, replace them with simpler alternatives. Vinegar and baking soda handle most household cleaning needs.

The Physical Systems: A Foundation Review

With an understanding of both occupational stress and environmental factors now established, let's turn to the systems themselves. Some of this will be review; some may be new. As you read, pay attention to what your body might be telling you. These systems don't fail in isolation – they're interconnected, and weakness in one often signals stress in others.

The Musculoskeletal System

Research into the impact of prolonged sitting – whether in a squad car, at a console, or behind a desk – reveals significant potential damage to bone and muscle health. For every two hours of continuous sitting, your risk of diabetes and obesity increases 5-7%. Simultaneously, remaining seated in a restricted environment increases stress to your back, neck, arms, and legs, potentially resulting in overstretched spinal ligaments and strained discs.

Your skeleton provides structure and protects vital organs, while bones serve as reservoirs for calcium and other minerals. The attached ligaments, tendons, and muscles enable movement, maintain posture, and generate heat. When this system is compromised – through trauma, overuse, postural strain, or prolonged immobilization – the pain can be debilitating.

People with significant musculoskeletal damage often describe a whole-body ache. Morning stiffness feels like their muscles are pulling. Even small amounts of activity feel overwhelming. Back pain is the second most common complaint reported to physicians, and for first responders who spend hours in physically restrictive positions, it's often a matter of when, not if.

The intervention is simple but requires consistency: do not let two hours pass without standing, moving, and stretching. Get out of the car, step away from the desk, and spend five minutes activating your body. Pay particular attention to your neck, shoulders, and trunk. This isn't luxury – it's maintenance that prevents catastrophic breakdown.

The Cardiovascular and Immune Systems

Nearly 50% of law enforcement officers will die from heart disease within five years of retirement. Read that again. You face a 25 times higher risk of death from cardiovascular disease than from any danger encountered on duty. While this research hasn't fully extended to all first response professions, the implications should be sobering regardless of your specific role.

Your cardiovascular system – heart and blood vessels – delivers oxygen and nutrients throughout your body while removing waste. Your lymphatic system, closely connected to cardiovascular health, removes toxins and produces immune cells. When these systems are functioning well, you have energy, resilience, and the capacity to recover from physical and emotional stress. When they're compromised, everything else starts to fail.

Six of the eight major risk factors for cardiovascular disease are within your control: smoking, sedentary lifestyle, obesity, high cholesterol, high blood pressure, and chronic stress. Only genetics and diabetes (though even diabetes is often preventable) fall outside your immediate influence.

Warning signs include shortness of breath during normal activity, fatigue that doesn't resolve with rest, chest pain or tightness, dizziness, irregular heartbeat, and unexplained pain in your neck, jaw, throat, or back. Immune system weakness shows up as recurrent infections, slow-healing wounds, persistent digestive trouble, and chronic fatigue.

The Nervous and Endocrine Systems

Your nervous system – brain and nerves – receives, stores, processes, and transmits information. It controls everything from heart rate and breathing to motor movement, sensory experience, and cognitive function. Your endocrine system works in partnership, serving as the gland command center and regulating hormone production and distribution.

Together, these systems govern your ability to assess danger, react appropriately, and navigate the fight-or-flight response that's so central to your work. When either system is compromised, the other suffers. Hormonal imbalance affects nervous system function; nervous system damage disrupts hormonal regulation.

For first responders, these systems take a particular beating. The constant cycling between high-alert and attempted recovery, combined with shift work that disrupts natural circadian rhythms, creates chronic dysfunction. Add the endocrine disruptors from environmental exposures, and you have a system under assault from multiple directions.

Symptoms of nervous system strain include confusion, difficulty processing information, loss of grip strength, and dizziness. Endocrine dysfunction often presents gradually: unexplained fatigue, weight fluctuation, mood instability, and disrupted sleep. Cushing's Syndrome – the result of chronic cortisol elevation – is increasingly common in first responders, characterized by fat accumulation between the shoulder blades, upper-body obesity despite normal eating, weakness, and high blood pressure.

The Digestive and Respiratory Systems

A sedentary lifestyle combined with poor food choices creates a perfect storm for digestive dysfunction. Your digestive system breaks food into usable nutrients and eliminates waste. When it's sluggish – from lack of movement, processed food intake, and alcohol consumption – the result is reflux, ulcers, gallstones, irritable bowel syndrome, and chronic constipation.

Your lungs provide oxygen necessary for cellular survival. Most respiratory problems stem from lifestyle choices: smoking (nicotine, marijuana, and e-cigarettes all cause damage), and surprisingly, a sedentary lifestyle. Prolonged sitting is associated with reduced pulmonary function, creating a vicious cycle where reduced lung capacity makes exercise more difficult, which leads to further deconditioning.

The fix for both systems is interconnected: movement and nutrition. Clean up what you're putting in, get your body moving regularly, and these systems begin to heal themselves. The digestive system in particular responds quickly to dietary changes – many people notice improved function within days of eliminating processed foods and increasing water intake.

Hydration

Your body is approximately 60% water. Every system depends on adequate hydration to function. Water regulates body temperature, maintains blood pressure, supports cognitive function, and facilitates every chemical reaction in your body. Chronic dehydration – which is remarkably common in first responders who limit fluid intake to avoid bathroom breaks – creates system-wide dysfunction.

But not all hydration is equal. As discussed earlier, water from plastic bottles carries its own risks. Soda is actively harmful. Even sports drinks, marketed as hydration solutions, are typically loaded with sugars, artificial colors, and chemicals.

The best hydration sources are filtered water (from glass or stainless-steel containers), naturally hydrating foods (fruits, vegetables, soups), and pure teas. A2 milk or goat milk provides excellent hydration alongside protein and nutrients. Coffee and tea contribute to hydration despite the caffeine, though be mindful of timing relative to sleep.

The occupational challenge is real: limited bathroom access discourages adequate fluid intake. But the consequences of chronic dehydration – reduced cognitive function, impaired physical performance, increased injury risk – are not abstract. They affect your ability to do your job safely. Find clean restrooms in your area, and make hydration a non-negotiable priority.

Sleep

Sleep is not optional. It's not a luxury. It's the single most powerful recovery tool available to you. The Centers for Disease Control recommends seven hours minimum for adults, with no more than 17 hours of continuous wakefulness. Exceed that threshold, and cognitive impairment begins to mirror intoxication.

Your profession is notoriously hostile to healthy sleep. Shift work disrupts circadian rhythms. Hypervigilance makes it difficult to downregulate. The images and experiences from duty follow you home. And the culture often celebrates pushing through fatigue rather than honoring the body's need for recovery.

But within this challenging context, there are factors you can control. Sleep hygiene – the practices and environment surrounding sleep – significantly impacts both sleep quality and duration.

Establish a consistent sleep schedule, even when your shifts vary. Your brain can adapt to non-traditional sleep times if you're consistent. Darken your bedroom completely – blackout curtains for day sleepers, removal of all light-emitting devices for everyone. Keep the temperature cool; bodies sleep better in cooler environments. Create a pre-sleep ritual that signals to your brain that it's time to wind down: the same activities in the same order, every time.

Equally important is what to avoid: no screens for two hours before sleep (the blue light suppresses melatonin), no caffeine within six hours, no intensive exercise within three hours, and no fast food or sugar close to bedtime. These substances activate your system precisely when you're trying to calm it.

The Power of Breath: Your Built-In Reset Button

Of all the physiological processes in your body, only one operates both automatically and under your conscious control: your breath. This isn't an accident – it's an evolutionary gift that gives you direct access to your nervous system's control panel.

When you're stressed, your breathing becomes shallow and rapid, which signals to your brain that danger is present, which releases more stress hormones, which makes your breathing even more shallow. It's a feedback loop that keeps you locked in a stress response even when the threat has passed.

But the loop works both ways. When you deliberately slow and deepen your breath, you send a powerful signal to your brain:

the danger has passed, it's safe to recover. Your parasympathetic nervous system activates, stress hormones begin to clear, and your body shifts from fight-or-flight into rest-and-repair.

The following breathwork techniques are tools you can use anywhere, anytime – in your cruiser, at your desk, before a difficult conversation, after a traumatic call. They require no equipment, no special training, and no one needs to know you're doing them.

Box Breathing (Tactical Reset)

This technique is used by Navy SEALs and elite athletes to maintain composure under extreme pressure. It's simple, discrete, and remarkably effective.

The pattern: Inhale through your nose for a count of 4. Hold your breath for a count of 4. Exhale through your mouth for a count of 4. Hold empty for a count of 4. Repeat.

Use it before difficult conversations, during stress spikes, or whenever you need to reset. Even two minutes of box breathing can significantly shift your physiological state.

The Physiological Sigh (30-Second Reset)

When you need the fastest possible nervous system reset, this technique delivers. Research from Stanford's Huberman Lab has shown it to be the single most effective breathing pattern for rapid stress reduction.

The pattern: Take a full inhale through your nose, then add a second short inhale to completely fill your lungs (a "top-off" breath). Follow with a long, slow exhale through your mouth – if you can comfortably extend it.

One or two cycles of this can shift your state when you don't have time for longer practice.

4-7-8 Breathing (Sleep Induction)

This pattern, developed by Dr. Andrew Weil, is specifically designed to activate the parasympathetic nervous system and prepare the body for sleep.

The pattern: Inhale through your nose for a count of 4. Hold for a count of 7. Exhale completely through your mouth for a count of 8. Repeat 3-4 times.

The extended exhale is key – it activates the vagus nerve and signals deep relaxation. This technique may feel strange at first, but effectiveness increases dramatically with regular practice.

Energizing Breath (Alertness Without Caffeine)

When you need to be sharp but you're dragging – and another cup of coffee isn't the answer – this technique provides a natural energy boost.

The pattern: Seated with a straight spine, take 20-30 rapid, rhythmic breaths through your nose (like a bellows). After the last exhale, take one deep breath in and hold for 15-30 seconds. Exhale and return to normal breathing.

This oxygenates your blood and activates your sympathetic nervous system naturally. Use it before shifts when you're tired, during long stretches of low activity, or anytime you need alertness without stimulants. Do not use before sleep.

Systems Check: Your Current Status

Before moving to the activities section, take a moment to honestly assess your current physical state. For each system, note any symptoms you're experiencing – whether at rest, at work, or under exertion. This isn't about judgment; it's about awareness. You can't address what you don't acknowledge.

Activities for Building Physical Capital

The activities below are organized using a 5-15-30 framework: quick wins you can implement immediately, deeper practices for when you have more time, and full engagement activities for dedicated wellness sessions. Start where you are. Build from there.

5-Minute Quick Wins

Try these today – no equipment or special preparation needed.

Body Scan on the Go: Right now, without changing your position, notice where you're holding tension. Shoulders up by your ears? Jaw clenched? Lower back compressed? Take three slow breaths, and with each exhale, consciously release one tension point. Congratulations – you just completed a body scan.

The 2-Hour Rule: Set a timer on your phone. Every two hours, stand up, reach toward the ceiling, twist gently at the waist in both directions, and roll your shoulders. Sixty seconds of movement can prevent hours of accumulated damage.

Water Audit: Look at what you've had to drink today. How many ounces of actual water – not coffee, not soda, not sports drinks? Whatever that number is, add eight more ounces before end of shift. Just start there.

Box Breathing Break: Before your next meal, before responding to that difficult email, or before walking into your house after shift: stop and do two minutes of box breathing. Notice how different you feel afterward.

Label Check: Pick up one product you use daily – shampoo, deodorant, lotion – and read the ingredient list. Just read it. Awareness is the first step.

15-Minute-Deep Practice

Set aside 15 minutes when you can be uninterrupted.

Systems Check-In with Breathwork: Sit comfortably and close your eyes. Complete five cycles of box breathing to settle your nervous system. Starting at the top of your head, mentally scan down through your body, noting any sensations – tension, discomfort, heaviness, ease. Without judgment, ask each area: "What do you need?" After completing the scan, write down what you noticed. Choose one action you can take in the next 24 hours to address what you heard.

Meal Prep Math: Write down what you spent on food delivery and fast-food last week. Calculate the annual equivalent. Look up one simple meal prep recipe that works with your schedule. Calculate the cost difference. Decide: is one meal prep session worth trying?

Product Audit: Go to your bathroom and examine the products you use every day. For each one, search the main ingredients online. What are you putting on your body? Make a list of products to replace when they run out.

Sleep Environment Assessment: Walk through your bedroom with fresh eyes. Is it dark enough? Cool enough? Are there screens or light-emitting devices? What's the last thing you do before attempting sleep? Write down three specific changes that would improve your sleep environment.

30-Minute Full Engagement

For your dedicated wellness time.

The Environmental Audit: Walk through your entire home examining water sources, body products, cleaning supplies, and food storage. For each category, identify what's potentially problematic and what's already clean. Create a prioritized "Switch List" of three items to replace with cleaner alternatives this month.

Kitchen Reset: Choose one 30-minute block to prepare proteins and vegetables for the week. Use glass containers for storage. Calculate what you just saved versus a week of delivery orders. Notice how you feel knowing clean food is ready when you need it.

Movement Inventory: Write down every form of physical movement you've engaged in over the past week – including walking, stretching, and physical work. Be honest. Then identify one form of movement you enjoy (or used to enjoy). What would it take to incorporate that into your next week? Schedule it like an appointment.

Breathwork Deep Dive: Spend 30 minutes learning and practicing the four breathwork techniques in this chapter. Start with box breathing (5 minutes), then try the physiological sigh (2 minutes), then 4-7-8 breathing (5 minutes), and finish with the energizing breath (3 minutes). Note which techniques feel most effective for you. Create a plan for when you'll use each one.

Closing Reflection

Physical capital isn't built in a single session or recovered after a single good night's sleep. It's accumulated through thousands of small choices – what you eat, what you drink, what you put on and in your body, how you move, how you breathe, how you rest. Every choice either deposits into or withdraws from your physical account.

The demands of your profession make these choices harder than they are for most people. Time is scarce. Stress is constant. Convenience is seductive. But the math is unforgiving: neglect your physical foundation, and everything else – your cognitive sharpness, emotional resilience, relationships, career longevity – suffers the consequences.

The good news is that your body wants to heal. Given half a chance – clean fuel, adequate rest, regular movement, reduced toxic load – it will begin repairing itself. The changes can start today. They can start with your next meal, your next glass of water, your next breath.

What will you choose?

Log Your Systems Checks in Your Journal

Musculoskeletal System Check: Note any pain, stiffness, or limitations – and whether they occur at rest, at work, or under exertion:

Cardiovascular & Immune System Check: Note any concerns – shortness of breath, fatigue, frequent illness, slow healing:

Nervous & Endocrine System Check: Note any confusion, mood instability, unexplained weight changes, or hormonal concerns:

Digestive & Respiratory System Check: Note any digestive issues, breathing difficulties, or related symptoms:

Hydration Check (24-hour audit): Track your fluid intake for one full day – type, amount, and timing:

Sleep Check: Describe your current sleep patterns, environment, and quality:

Environmental Exposure Check: Note products and exposures you've identified for change:

Chapter Three

Psychological Capital: The Mindset Foundation

Adversity: Depression & Hopelessness

Before we go any further in this book, you need to know something that changes everything: the attitudes that determine whether you thrive or deteriorate in this profession are not fixed. They can be developed. They can be trained. They can be strengthened.

This might seem obvious, but it's not how most people think about psychological wellness. We tend to believe that some people are just naturally resilient, naturally optimistic, naturally able to handle stress – and others aren't. We look at colleagues who seem unaffected by the job and assume they're built differently.

They're not. Or rather, the differences aren't genetic destiny. Research has definitively shown that the psychological characteristics that predict who thrives under pressure can be deliberately developed. This chapter explains what those characteristics are and how to build them. It's the foundation everything else in this book rests on.

The most authentic thing about us is our capacity to create, to overcome, to endure, to transform, to love, and to be greater than our suffering.

– Ben Okri

The Adversity That Steals Everything

Depression is the adversity most closely connected to this chapter – and it's particularly sinister because it attacks the very capacity that would help you fight it.

Depression doesn't just make you sad. It convinces you that nothing will help. It tells you that effort is pointless, that change is impossible, that you're fundamentally broken in ways that can't be fixed. It steals hope – and without hope, you stop trying.

According to culturally competent treatment facilities serving first responders, the most common depression symptoms in this population include:

- Extreme fatigue or persistent exhaustion that sleep doesn't fix
- Loss of enthusiasm – dreading work you once loved
- Unfair self-blame for things beyond your control
- Loss of confidence in your decision-making
- Feeling hopeless about the future and disconnected from purpose

Warning signs include appetite changes, irritability, concentration problems, sleep disruption, withdrawal from activities you used to enjoy, and – critically – thoughts of suicide.

In psychological autopsies conducted after first responder suicides, the most common precursor isn't trauma exposure or even PTSI. It's hopelessness. The belief that things will never get better. The loss of the future.

This is why understanding psychological capital matters so much. It's the antidote to hopelessness – and it can be built.

A critical note: not everything that looks like depression *is* depression. Research published in the *Journal of Neuropsychiatry and Clinical Neurosciences* distinguishes between depression – which involves emotional pain and hopelessness – and apathy, which involves feeling nothing at all. The person with depression feels sad; the person with apathy feels empty. Similarly, a 2024 study in *Scientific Reports* confirmed that boredom, while highly related to depression, "is not simply a milder form of depression, but represents a distinct state." And purposelessness – the loss of meaning and mission – is a *pathway* to depression, not depression itself.

Why does this distinction matter? Because the interventions differ. Depression may require clinical treatment. Apathy responds to meaningful goals and challenges. Boredom requires increased stimulation, not rest. Purposelessness requires reconnection to mission. The psychological capital framework addresses all of these – but knowing which condition you're facing helps you target your effort.

If You're Struggling Now

> If you're experiencing depression symptoms – especially hopelessness or thoughts of suicide – please don't wait to seek help.
>
> 988 Suicide & Crisis Lifeline (call or text)
>
> Safe Call Now: 1-206-459-3020 (24/7, first responder specific)

The fact that you're reading this book suggests you haven't given up. That matters. Help exists, and it works.

What Separates Those Who Thrive

For decades, researchers asked a simple question: Why do some people – regardless of the challenges they face – continue to grow and perform at high levels while others deteriorate into apathy, addiction, and hopelessness?

The initial hypothesis was that skills and knowledge made the difference. Train people better, give them more information, and they'll perform better. But this didn't hold up. Some highly trained people collapsed under pressure while others with less training thrived.

The breakthrough came when researchers shifted focus from what people knew to how people thought. The answer wasn't skills – it was attitudes. Specifically, four psychological characteristics that consistently separate high performers from everyone else.

These four characteristics were named Positive Psychological Capital – PsyCap for short.

The Heroes Project

The research foundation for this book comes from the HEROES Project – a multi-year study of over 10,000 first responders examining whether PsyCap could be trained and whether that training would reduce psychological injury.

- Results from participants who completed the Navigating Adversity training:
- 68% improvement in overall wellness
- 36% increase in positive PsyCap scores

- 32% decrease in mental distress symptoms
- 26% reduction in depression
- 28% reduction in anxiety
- 34% reduction in stress

Perhaps most striking: Of participants who began training with severe PTSI symptoms, 100% ended with normal scores.

This isn't motivational rhetoric. This is validated research showing that psychological capital can be built – and that building it creates measurable protection against the adversities you'll face.

The Four Pillars of Psychological Capital

PsyCap consists of four interconnected characteristics. Each can be developed independently, but they're most powerful when built together.

The Foundation Beneath the Foundation

Before we go further, you need to understand something about yourself.

Research in mission-critical professions has identified 10 psychological skills that predict exceptional performance under pressure: social competence, teamwork, adaptability, conscientiousness, impulse control, integrity, emotional regulation, decision-making, assertiveness, and avoiding self-destructive behaviors.

These 10 skills are present in roughly 4% of the population. You almost certainly possess most or all of them – it's part of what brought you to this work.

But here's the crucial distinction: for the 4%, these aren't skills you consciously deploy. They're your *default response* under pressure. When crisis hits, you don't think "I need to regulate my emotions now" – you just regulate. When split-second decisions are required, you don't run through a decision-making framework – you assess and act.

This is both your greatest asset and your greatest vulnerability.

The asset: you function where others fail.

The vulnerability: because these skills feel automatic, it's easy to forget they require maintenance. You can neglect what seems to happen naturally – until the day it doesn't happen anymore. The default weakens. The automatic becomes effortful. The instinctive requires conscious thought.

The Psychological Capital you'll build in this chapter sits on top of these 10 skills. PsyCap – hope, efficacy, resilience, optimism – is the framework for maintaining and strengthening what you already possess. It's not about learning new skills. It's about keeping your default response sharp.

Hope: The Strategic Engine

Hope, as defined in psychological research, isn't wishful thinking or passive optimism. It's a cognitive system with two components: willpower (the determination to pursue goals) and waypower (the ability to generate pathways to achieve them).

High-hope individuals don't just want things to be different – they create specific plans to make them different. When one path is blocked, they generate alternatives. They think strategically about the future rather than just hoping for the best.

In first responder context, hope looks like:

- Having a clear vision of where you want to be professionally and personally

- Breaking large goals into achievable milestones
- Developing contingency plans before you need them
- Maintaining forward momentum even when progress is slow

Hope is the antidote to the hopelessness that precedes depression and suicide. When you have a future worth pursuing and paths to get there, the present – no matter how difficult – becomes bearable.

> **FIELD PERSPECTIVE**
>
> *"Five years in, I was completely stuck. Same rank, same assignment, same frustration. A mentor asked me to write down where I wanted to be in five years and work backward. Just having that vision – and actual steps to get there – changed everything. I wasn't stuck anymore. I was on a path."*
>
> **– Detective, 12 years of service**

Self-Efficacy: The Confidence to Execute

Self-efficacy isn't general confidence – it's task-specific belief in your ability to succeed at particular challenges. It's the conviction that you have the skills, resources, and determination to accomplish what you set out to do.

High self-efficacy doesn't mean you think everything is easy. It means you believe that with sufficient effort and the right approach, you can overcome obstacles. You see challenges as problems to solve rather than evidence of your inadequacy.

Self-efficacy develops through four mechanisms:

- Mastery experiences – Successfully accomplishing challenging tasks

- Vicarious learning – Watching someone like you succeed
- Verbal persuasion – Encouragement from people you respect
- Physiological state management – Interpreting stress as readiness rather than fear

In first responder contexts, self-efficacy looks like tackling difficult assignments rather than avoiding them, viewing setbacks as learning opportunities, and maintaining effort when outcomes are uncertain.

FROM THE COMM CENTER

"Every time I took on a call type I was scared of – working the active shooter, the CPR in progress with a kid – and handled it, my confidence grew. Not because I was perfect, but because I learned I could handle imperfect. Now I volunteer for the hard stuff because that's where I grow."

– 911 Telecommunicator, 6 years of service

Optimism: The Interpretive Lens

Optimism in the PsyCap framework isn't about being positive all the time or ignoring reality. It's about how you interpret events – particularly setbacks and successes.

Optimists attribute negative events to temporary, specific, and external causes: "This situation is difficult right now, but it will pass." They attribute positive events to permanent, pervasive, and personal causes: "My effort made this happen, and it will continue to pay off."

Pessimists do the opposite. They see negative events as permanent and personal ("I'm a failure") and positive events as temporary and external ("I just got lucky").

The practical difference is enormous. Optimistic attribution keeps you moving forward when things go wrong and builds confidence when things go right. Pessimistic attribution creates learned helplessness – the belief that nothing you do matters.

Developing optimism involves:

- Catching yourself when you make permanent/personal attributions for setbacks
- Deliberately reframing temporary/specific interpretations
- Giving yourself appropriate credit for successes
- Using positive self-talk, especially under pressure

Realistic Optimism

- Healthy optimism isn't denial. It's not pretending everything is fine when it isn't.
- Realistic optimism means:
- Acknowledging the real difficulty of challenges
- Believing in your capacity to handle them anyway
- Focusing on what you can control
- Committing to effort over outcome

Resilience: The Recovery System

Resilience is the most discussed and most misunderstood of the four pillars. It's not about avoiding difficulty or being unaffected by trauma. It's about how you respond to adversity – and what you become afterward.

The definition used in this book: Resilience is a person's intentional recovery from failure, setback, conflict, or even positive change, landing in a stronger strategic position than before.

Note the key word: intentional. Resilience isn't just bouncing back – it's deliberately learning from adversity, so you're better prepared for the next challenge. It requires honest evaluation: What happened? What did I do well? What would I do differently? What can I take from this?

Resilience develops through:

- Altering risk levels – Deliberately exposing yourself to manageable challenges
- Activating positive emotions – Building reserves through gratitude, connection, and meaning
- Fostering self-development – Continuously building skills and knowledge
- Honest evaluation – Reviewing setbacks with trusted advisors

Research originally suggested resilience was a fixed trait – something you either had or didn't. We now know it's a developable capacity. The more you deliberately practice recovery from adversity, the more resilient you become.

FIELD PERSPECTIVE

"After the shooting, I could have just buried it and moved on. Instead, I asked my sergeant to walk through the scene with me weeks later. We broke down every second. What I did right, what I could have done better, what was just bad luck. That conversation was harder than the shooting itself – but it's why I'm still on the job instead of drinking myself to sleep."

– Officer, 9 years of service

PsyCap as Protection

Here's what makes psychological capital so important for first responders: it's inversely associated with virtually every adversity you'll face.

High levels of PsyCap are correlated with lower rates of:

- Depression
- Anxiety
- Chronic stress
- Post-traumatic stress injury
- Burnout
- Even physical conditions like hypertension and heart disease

This isn't because PsyCap prevents bad things from happening. It's because PsyCap changes how you process and recover from difficult experiences. The same traumatic call affects a high-PsyCap responder differently than a low-PsyCap responder – not because they feel it less, but because they have better tools for integration and recovery.

Perhaps most importantly, PsyCap is protective against the comorbidity that makes first responder mental health so complicated. When someone struggles with PTSI, there's an 80% chance they're also dealing with depression, anxiety, addiction, or other compounding conditions. Building PsyCap doesn't just address one adversity – it builds resistance across the entire spectrum.

Beyond Clinical Depression

This protective effect extends to conditions that mimic depression. The hope pillar directly counters purposelessness by rebuilding vision and pathways. The self-efficacy pillar activates the goal-directed motivation that apathy suppresses. The combination of challenge-seeking and mastery experiences provides the stimulation that boredom requires. In other words, PsyCap training may be helping first responders recover from conditions that were never clinical depression in the first place – which partly explains why the HEROES Project showed such dramatic results.

The Compound Effect

The four PsyCap characteristics don't just add together – they multiply.

Hope provides direction: Where are you going?

Self-Efficacy provides confidence: Can you get there?

Resilience provides learning: What do you do when you stumble?

Optimism provides fuel: Why keep going?

Each pillar strengthens the others. As your hope increases, your efficacy grows. As your efficacy grows, your resilience improves. As your resilience improves, your optimism rises. As your optimism rises, your hope expands.

This is why small improvements in PsyCap can produce large improvements in overall wellbeing – and why the HEROES Project showed such significant results.

Why This Chapter Comes Early

You might wonder why we're covering psychological capital before discussing specific adversities like PTSI, anxiety, or organizational stress. The reason is foundational: everything else in this book builds on the premise that you can change.

If you believe your psychological characteristics are fixed – that you're either resilient or you're not, optimistic or you're not – then the rest of this book becomes a diagnostic tool at best. You'll read about adversities and either recognize yourself or not, but you won't believe you can do anything about it.

But if you understand that hope, self-efficacy, resilience, and optimism are trainable capacities – that they can be deliberately developed regardless of where you're starting from – then every chapter that follows becomes an opportunity. The adversities aren't just things that happen to you; they're challenges you can prepare for and recover from.

This shift in understanding – from fixed to developable – is itself a form of psychological capital. It's the growth mindset that makes everything else possible.

FROM THE COMM CENTER

"I always thought some people were just built for this job and I wasn't one of them. Learning that resilience is a skill, not a trait, changed everything. I stopped waiting to feel better and started practicing getting better. Three years later, I'm training new dispatchers and actually enjoying the job."

– Communications Training Officer, 8 years of service

Activities for Building Psychological Capital

PsyCap is built through deliberate practice. These activities target each pillar while recognizing that they reinforce each other.

When you experience low energy, loss of interest, or emotional flatness, does it feel more like sadness and hopelessness (depression), or more like emptiness and "nothing matters" (apathy), or more like restlessness and understimulation (boredom)? Your answer may point to which PsyCap pillar needs the most attention.

5-Minute Reflection: Your Default Under Pressure

Think of a recent high-pressure situation where you performed well.

- Which of your psychological skills activated automatically?
- Did any skills feel more effortful than they used to?
- What might be eroding without your awareness?

The goal isn't to learn to deploy these skills – you already do that naturally. The goal is to notice which ones might be weakening so you can target your maintenance efforts.

5-Minute Quick Wins

Small practices that build momentum.

The Future Vision (Hope): Close your eyes and imagine yourself two years from now, thriving. What's different? What did you accomplish? What does your daily life look like? Spend just two minutes with this vision. Having a clear picture of where you're going activates the hope system.

The Win Log (Self-Efficacy): At the end of each shift, write down one thing you handled well. Not perfectly – just competently. Building a record of small wins trains your brain to recognize your own capability.

The Reframe (Optimism): When something goes wrong, catch your first interpretation. Is it permanent ('This always happens') or temporary ('This is a difficult moment')? Personal ('I'm a failure') or specific ('This situation is challenging')? Practice shifting toward temporary and specific.

The Learning Question (Resilience): After any difficult experience, ask yourself: What's one thing I can take from this? Not 'what did I do wrong' but 'what did I learn?' This simple reframe turns setbacks into development.

15-Minute-Deep Practice

For focused PsyCap development.

The Pathways Exercise (Hope): Choose a goal you're working toward. Write down three different ways you could achieve it. Then for each pathway, identify what could go wrong and how you'd adapt. High-hope thinking isn't about one perfect plan – it's about multiple routes to the same destination.

The Roadblock Inventory (Self-Efficacy): List the obstacles standing between you and a goal. For each one, identify whether it's a challenge (requiring your own effort) or a barrier (requiring help from others). Then list specific resources you could bring to bear on each. This converts vague anxiety into actionable planning.

The Attribution Audit (Optimism): Think of a recent success and a recent setback. For each, write down how you explained it to yourself. Did you take appropriate credit for the success? Did you make the setback more permanent/personal than it needed to be? Adjust your attributions consciously.

The After-Action Review (Resilience): Choose a difficult experience from the past week. Write: What happened? What went well? What would I do differently? What can I carry forward? This structured reflection is how resilience is deliberately built.

30-Minute Full Engagement

For comprehensive psychological development.

The Strategic Plan (Hope): Identify one significant goal in your life – professional, physical, relational, financial. Define it specifically and set a timeline. Then work backward: What milestones would indicate progress? What are the first three steps? When will you take them? Document this plan and review it weekly.

The Mastery Challenge (Self-Efficacy): Identify one skill you've been avoiding because it feels too hard. Commit to practicing it for 30 minutes. Not mastering it – just engaging with it. The goal isn't perfection; it's proof that you can tackle difficult things. Each mastery experience builds efficacy for the next challenge.

The Gratitude & Progress Review (Optimism): Write down three things you're grateful for, three things you've accomplished recently (no matter how small), and three things you're looking forward to. This structured positivity practice counteracts the negativity bias that undermines optimism.

The Trusted Advisor Debrief (Resilience): Schedule time with someone you trust – a colleague, mentor, or friend. Walk through a difficult experience together. Ask for honest feedback: What did they observe? What would they have done differently? What strengths did they see you demonstrate? External perspective is essential for building resilience.

The Caveat: You Have to Do the Work

The research is clear: psychological capital can be developed, and developing it creates measurable protection against the adversities you'll face.

But here's the caveat that no training program can remove: You have to do the work.

Reading about PsyCap doesn't build PsyCap. Understanding the concepts doesn't create capacity. Only practice – deliberate, consistent, ongoing practice – builds the psychological capital that protects you.

Chapter Three Reflection

Consider these questions honestly. Your answers are for you alone.

- Where would you rate yourself on each PsyCap pillar right now? (1-10)

  Hope: _____ Self-Efficacy: _____

  Optimism: _____ Resilience: _____

- Which pillar feels most developed? Which needs the most attention?
- What goal do you have that could serve as a focus for building hope?
- What's a recent setback, and how did you interpret it? Was that interpretation helpful?
- Who in your life could serve as a trusted advisor for building resilience?
- What one PsyCap-building practice will you commit to this week.

Chapter Four

Rodger's Triggering Incident

Before you read this chapter, we want you to understand why it's here.

Throughout this book, we'll present research, frameworks, and practical tools for building resilience. All of that matters. But wellness isn't built on abstractions – it's built on the hard-won wisdom of people who've walked through fire and found their way back. Rodger's story is that kind of wisdom.

What follows is a detailed account of the incident that triggered Rodger's post-traumatic stress injury, the years of unrecognized suffering that followed, and his eventual path to complete recovery. We share it for three reasons:

To show you that even the most severe psychological injuries can heal

To help you recognize warning signs you might be dismissing in yourself

To demonstrate that seeking help – despite the professional risks – is the only path to genuine recovery

Rodger tells his story in his own words. It's raw. It's uncomfortable. And for some readers, it may stir up memories of your own. If that happens, pause. Use the breathing techniques from Chapter Two. Give yourself permission to read this in stages if needed.

His story is not included to frighten you. It's included because it's true, because it ends in hope, and because someone like Rodger – fully recovered and thriving – is living proof that there is no darkness so deep that you can't find your way out.

A Note Before Reading

> This chapter contains detailed descriptions of a fatal accident scene, including graphic imagery. If you're currently struggling with trauma symptoms, consider whether now is the right time to read this.
>
> If difficult emotions arise while reading, try this grounding technique: Name 5 things you can see, 4 things you can hear, 3 things you can touch, 2 things you can smell, and 1 thing you can taste. Breathe slowly. You are safe. You are here.
>
> If you need support, the resources at the end of this book can help

Santa Rosa, California – 1995

"Six Mary One priority detail," came the call at the end of both my shift and work week".

"Mary One," I answered, glancing over at the officer in the car next to me. He was with me working on his traffic accident investigation skills which, at the time, was my particular field of expertise.

"Mary One, respond to a major injury accident, multiple vehicles involved, Stonypoint and Hearn. Fire and paramedics responding."

"Mary One, 10-4, responding code 3." The exhaustion seemed to overwhelm my entire body. It had been a long week with added training responsibilities, and all I wanted to do was get home to my family, have

a nice meal, and spend time relaxing over the weekend. But that was not to be."

"Mary One, be advised we are receiving multiple calls on this accident. It appears there are several vehicles involved and several people are injured. Additional fire and ambulance personnel are responding."

Hearing those words signaled my sense of duty and initiated the adrenaline of anticipation. The fatigue melted away and, in its place, I could feel my senses sharpen and my focus home in on each detail as it was relayed over the radio. My partner and I rolled code three to the call.

"Mary One, copy. ETA two minutes."

My response was followed by a tone alert, which was reserved for the most serious calls. Its use signaled that everyone working needed to hear the information that would follow. The sound of that tone triggered an even bigger dump of adrenalin...something I loved and dreaded at the same time."

"Any unit in the area of Stonypoint and Hearn, respond to that location code three to assist with a major accident. Mary One, be advised, we are now receiving information that there may be multiple fatalities. Fire will be staging and beginning triage operations as well as setting up an incident command."

I could hear the distress in the dispatcher's voice. That was highly unusual because this dispatcher had been working in the 911 emergency call center for a couple of decades and was always calm, cool, and collected. She was a virtual eye in the midst of a storm. Our city rocked-and-rolled pretty well most of the time, so hearing the anxiety in her tone of voice added to my growing sense of dread, which seemed to push my body's chemical response into overdrive. This was obviously a critical incident that would need significant resources. I buried the gas pedal.

"Mary One copy. Sixty seconds out."

I willed my patrol car to go faster as I sped to the call weaving in and out of traffic. I felt my entire system enter the zone of peak performance...a place where the adrenaline and cortisol mixed into a serum of superhuman strength and focus. I lived for that feeling. I needed it like a junkie needs heroin.

RODGER'S REFLECTION

Looking back, I can see how addicted I was to that chemical surge. The job trains you to chase it – and rewards you when you do. What I didn't understand then was that my nervous system was paying a price every time I flooded it with those stress hormones. I was making withdrawals from an account I didn't know had a limit.

I watched the firefighters on the scene take one of the rear doors off the vehicle and remove an infant, still strapped in a car seat. They immediately covered the child with a yellow tarp. I was aghast! How could they cover a sleeping child with a tarp like that? I yelled at them, demanding that they see to the infant's needs. They looked at me like I was insane. Again, my mind created a perceptual distortion – this time to protect me from witnessing the baby's physical trauma. The child was beyond saving, a truth that was obvious to everyone except me.

I turned away, admitting that I was useless to the firefighters, but knowing that I was needed in other ways. Nearly every officer, paramedic, EMT and firefighter in the entire city was arriving on scene. The noise of the sirens, traffic, power tools, emergency personnel yelling orders, and screams of the injured filled the air. The sound was deafening, overwhelming me, and for a moment I felt utterly hopeless. My usually large and in charge personality completely disintegrated and everything I knew myself capable of vanished.

One of the sergeants on the scene noticed me standing there like a deer in the headlights. He asked me, a bit incredulously, what I was doing. I was completely honest and told him I had no idea what to do, so he told me to take some photographs of the scene before all the emergency personnel destroyed key evidence. I remember being so grateful to have a task to focus on, and a way to put my immense stress response to use.

Although I was physically shaking, I did manage to take photographs that later turned out to be some of the most valuable evidence gathered that day. Little did I know those pictures would trigger a massive release of my post-traumatic stress injury, an injury that began building in the unconscious recesses of my mind, years before.

The Long Investigation

I remained on that scene for an additional twenty hours while we did our investigative work on the accident. I drank a pot of coffee to keep my energy up, which gave me some serious jitters when mixed with the stress hormone cocktail. I helped process the three fatalities with the coroner by taking detailed photographs. I collected bloody evidence and helped clean up body parts and debris to clear the roadway. I assisted in measuring the crime scene roadway, vehicles, and bodies. I conducted interviews with witnesses who were in various stages of shock, urging them to go over, in excruciating detail, every nuance of what they could recall. With each new account, I felt a shadow of my own trauma lingering in the back of my mind, reliving the day over and over again. I visited victims at different hospitals who experienced various degrees of trauma. I thought it would never end. When the picture of what had happened began to take shape, I realized the whole accident was completely avoidable.

It all began with a minor hit-and-run accident. The van driver backed into a parked car in a parking lot, inflicting minor damage to a vehicle. The man then left the scene without notifying anyone of the accident. A witness to the accident decided to follow the van, planning to report the crime he had witnessed. The driver of the van, later determined to be driving under the influence of alcohol, realized that he was being followed, and sped away. The witness, under the influence of methamphetamine, chased. This "pursuit" went on for over seven miles, often reaching speeds in excess of 100 miles per hour, with their vehicles weaving in and out of traffic, crossing into the opposing lanes, and passing cars on the shoulder of the roadway.

When the chase reached the intersection of Stonypoint and Hearn, the driver of the van ran the red light and hit the first vehicle – the one I thought I saw my daughters inside of – killing the woman and infant. The van then flipped into the air, upside down. Because it was a conversion van, the top flew off midair. The driver fell out of the van, which then landed on the driver, killing a third person. With continued momentum, the van rolled end-over-end, smashing tops of the other cars involved in the accident. In total eight cars were crashed, and fifteen people were injured.

By the time I went home, I was beyond exhausted. My shift had started at 0700 the day before and, because of the pileup, continued for twenty-eight hours beyond its scheduled end. My forty-hour work week became nearly seventy. The adrenaline, caffeine, and cortisol refused to abate enough to allow for sleep, so I stayed awake – replaying over and over in my mind the hallucination of seeing my daughters in the backseat of that car. I tried to push it away, but I could not stop this nightmare from taking over my life. It was as if someone else was in charge of the movie reel that was my brain and it continued to play on repeat, making me feel like I was unraveling mentally and physically.

It was supposed to be my weekend, but due to the scale of the event and my role as a traffic accident investigator, my days off were canceled. I went back to work to begin what would become a three-week investigation. Each day, with witness after witness, I went over every detail again and again and again.

We filed manslaughter charges and driving-under-the-influence charges against the civilian who chased the driver of the van. The district attorney refused to pursue the case because he did not believe there was enough evidence to prove either charge, despite our exhaustive investigation. I felt a sense of righteous indignation, followed by a chaser of resentment and a fist full of betrayal. The system failed. Again.

It was not the first time in my career that I struggled with accepting an imperfect justice system. I did my best to let it go and tried to tell myself that I had done everything I could do to ensure a just outcome, then went back to my regular duties as a motor officer. Life went on but something about me was changed. I could not put my finger on what it was exactly, but I could sense something was different...and as time passed, that something got worse.

Five Years Later: The Breaking Point

The civil trial for one of the defendants in the original accident was set. Even though five years had passed, the wheels of justice still turned slowly and it was finally time for the deposition that would determine how much money he would have to pay as his share of the carnage his actions caused. I was in my fifteenth year as a police officer by then, and quite comfortable with the deposition process. Part of the procedure is the recounting of the events of that day, which I prepared for by reading the entire report ahead of time.

I stepped into the office where the deposition was held to see a host of people sitting around a beautiful, long, highly-polished mahogany table. The scene reminded me of a legal television drama. The judge was joined by eighteen civil attorneys representing the various people involved in the accident. Knowing that everyone wanted my testimony to support a specific side of events, I felt like chum in a shark tank.

I sat down to a stack of the photographs. It turns out, they were the pictures I took of the crime scene. One-by-one, I was asked to go over each photo and describe what I saw. I picked up the first photograph and, of course, it was the first car I approached that day – the one that I saw my daughters in.

Without warning, I was consumed by a total and complete flashback. Mentally, I left that office and returned to the accident. Instead of the attorneys' cologne and wood polish, I smelled the viscera. In the place of lawyerly mutterings, I heard whimpering, sobbing, and screaming. The sound of sirens filled the air and everywhere I looked was chaos.

My mouth went dry. My hands shook violently. My shirt was soaked through with sweat. I desperately struggled to not piss my pants as wave after wave of sensations catapulted me into the past.

When the flashback subsided, I had no idea how much time had passed. The mental fog cleared to reveal the judge and attorneys all looking at me in shock and disbelief. I was crying. I do not remember starting to cry, but the tears falling down my face were real enough. Again, reality failed me, leaving me deeply confused and horribly disoriented. My inability to grasp what was real in the moment and what was memory was probably the worst part of the experience. In my struggle to breathe, I shoved my chair back and walked out of the room without a word. Thankfully, no one tried to stop me.

When I stepped outside, I was greeted by a bright, sunny, spring day. I remember the warmth of the sun on my face, something I find still brings me comfort. Standing there, breathing in the fresh air, I realized that I was in trouble and admitted that I needed help. I found the number to our employee assistance program and made the dreaded call to set an appointment with a police psychologist.

RODGER'S REFLECTION

That moment outside – sun on my face, fresh air in my lungs – was the turning point. I couldn't pretend anymore. Something was deeply wrong, and I finally accepted that I couldn't fix it alone. That admission was the hardest thing I'd ever done. It was also the beginning of getting my life back.

The Stigma of Seeking Help

In the late 1990's, our psychological services program was fairly new. We were permitted six anonymous visits to a culturally competent police psychologist without having to notify the administration. If the psychologist believed that more was needed, officers had to request approval for additional sessions. Unfortunately, this meant admitting the need for psychological help, one of the ramifications of which was career suicide.

Just going to see a psychologist was dangerous to a person's reputation because people would start to wonder if they could trust you. As a department, we were trying to transition away from the old-school suck it up mentality and toward a more supportive culture, but psychological services still existed as a box check. We could say that counseling services were available, but we had not yet evolved to the point where we could overcome the stigma attached to needing a police psychologist. At that point in my career, I no longer cared what people thought. I could not keep up the façade that everything was okay. I was going to get some help regardless of the consequences.

On the day of my first appointment, I parked three blocks away from the psychiatrist's office, wore a disguise, and walked around the block twice – just to make sure that no one from the department would see me. When I was nearing the building, I literally ran inside to avoid detection.

Let that image settle for a moment: a veteran officer, respected in his department, so afraid of being seen entering a therapist's office that he wore a disguise and ran to avoid detection. That was the culture. In many places, it still is.

From the beginning of therapy, I knew I had made the right choice in coming. My therapist was a thirty-year practitioner who had treated dozens of police personnel from various departments in our area. She understood me and she understood the job.

The Hidden Danger

Because she understood, our time together revealed something I had never consciously acknowledged: in the five years since Stonypoint and Hearn, I had transitioned away from the safety-first, by-the-book cop I had been into one who actively, almost daily, tried to kill myself. Not consciously, but it was clear that the changes to my behavior were driven by suicidal ideation. Surprisingly, my reaction to trauma was not unique. An incredibly high number of police and first responders live in the shadow of the past, reacting to it by doing exactly what I did.

I wanted to take myself out in a blaze of glory.

After the critical incident, I began to rush into danger. I violated policies and procedures constantly. The safety conscious officer I had always been gave way to what I thought was a courageous hero. In truth, I was totally reckless and not only placed myself in danger, but also my partners and the community I served. Oddly, and in complete opposition to what should have happened, I kept winning. Everything I did worked out so well that I started to believe I was invincible.

My bosses noticed the behavior change, knew I was violating policy and procedure to bring home these huge wins, yet their reaction was completely positive. I was given awards and commendations. No one called me out for being irresponsible. Instead, I became the quintessential heroic officer, praised and admired by all. In honor of my bravado, my peers honored me with the nickname "Street monster." Work morphed into a daily game of chicken, with the prize notoriety bordering on fame, and the penalty for losing, death.

RODGER'S REFLECTION

The culture rewarded the very behaviors that were destroying me. Awards for recklessness. Admiration for danger-seeking. A nickname that celebrated what was actually a slow-motion suicide attempt. If anyone had understood what was really happening, they would have pulled me off the street immediately. But we didn't have the language or the awareness to see it for what it was.

My behavior at work naturally overlapped into my personal life. I sought out high-risk activities to fuel my ever-growing need for that rush of adrenaline. I did full-contact fighting as a martial artist. I sought physical fights whenever possible with civilians in my off-duty time who I judged to be assholes, often under the influence of liquid courage. I rode with breakneck speed on my mountain bike down single-track trails. I even road-raced motorcycles as an amateur at Sears Point International Raceway and on the mountain roads in my community. I was out of control, but I just kept winning no matter how hard or how far I pushed life's envelope.

The Diagnosis and the Choice

At the conclusion of my allowable six sessions in therapy, I was diagnosed with the most severe case of post-traumatic stress disorder my therapist had ever seen in thirty years of practice. This latest label was not an achievement I wanted, but it gave me a starting point. A problem to solve, which led to my next big decision. To remain in therapy, I had to request approval from my department administration.

I now had to decide between career suicide versus actual suicide.

In my condition, the choice was obvious. Not only did I have a wife, two beautiful children, and a strong desire to live, I was willing to pursue recovery without regard for the professional consequences. My therapist told me that she wanted me to consider a new, experimental therapy. Because of its relative youth, there was little known about how or why the therapeutic technique was so successful, but she knew that it was getting some excellent results for people struggling with PTSD. I agreed to try it, sought and received departmental approval, and became one of the first people in America to receive Eye Movement Desensitization and Reprocessing (EMDR) – a therapy that today is considered the gold-standard in healing post-traumatic stress injuries.

Recovery

I completed six sessions of EMDR with profound results. While the reason for my therapy focused on the events that occurred at Stonypoint and Hearn, I quickly discovered that I was also living with wounds from six other critical incidents. These were events I had not thought about in years: the nurse who died in my arms after being hit by a bus, the drunk who hit a tree and died in my arms while I was trying to free him from the wreckage of his burning car, the gang banger who was stabbed seven times in the upper body with three sucking chest wounds who fought me as I saved his life, the man who stabbed himself over and over in the abdomen with a machete after being on a three-day methamphetamine binge while I tried to talk him into peaceful surrender, the sniper whose shot went just above my head, the round embedding in a telephone pole I was standing next to, and the men I fought hand-to-hand to the death as their hearts exploded from excited delirium brought on by toxic levels of methamphetamine.

My brain masked those critical incidents to protect me from their ruthlessness, but they were there, simmering, waiting for release. Because of the number of buried traumas I was living with, my diagnosis was updated to Complex Post-Traumatic Stress Disorder (C-PTSD).

When EMDR revealed the stacked nature of the traumatic experiences in my mind, I was surprised but relieved, too. The therapy was working, and I could feel a return to my normal self. I could recall the incident with excellent clarity, but the emotional charge surrounding the entire traumatic experience was gone. I went back to being the safe, by-the-book officer I was before the incident. I was sleeping well again and had a healthy relationship with my wife and kids once again. I gave up many of my adrenaline-centric behaviors and started to actively seek a balanced, resilient life.

By taking control of my wellness, I was able to exert influence over the way I handled future incidents. I was no longer afraid of the unknown, nor of the memories of what had been. Instead, I learned to embrace adversity with a newly found confidence that the tools I was learning would help keep me healthy, happy, and safe from ever returning to the negative coping behaviors that would have eventually resulted in my death.

The Professional Cost – And What It Was Worth

I felt such joy at the end of my last therapy session because I felt normal again and it was an amazing feeling. I did not have to carry the heavy burden of trauma anymore. I was free and that feeling was worth whatever price I had to pay professionally.

When I returned to work, many of my brothers and sisters in uniform hesitated to trust me. They feared that, when bullets started flying, I would become a liability on the street. Eventually though, they realized that I was stronger for the psychological work I did, which made me even more dependable than I was before. My career, regarding promotion, was over. The stigma of seeking psychological services at that time in the profession's history was simply too strong to rebound from. I did not allow that to stop me from doing what I was called to do. I loved being in the patrol division and I thrived as a perishable skills instructor.

RODGER'S REFLECTION

Would I make the same choice today? In a heartbeat. The promotion I lost was nothing compared to what I gained: my life, my family, my peace of mind. The officers who initially doubted me eventually became some of my strongest supporters. They saw what recovery looked like, and some of them quietly asked me how to find the same help. Every one of those conversations made the professional cost worth it.

Injury, Not Disorder

In the first-response culture, we like to label ourselves. No one says, "I'm professional staff for the city of..." or "I practice law enforcement for the city of..." Instead, we say, "I'm a police officer" or "I'm a 911 dispatcher." We love those labels. They are badges of honor.

Being labeled with a disorder, though, is a completely different matter. Disorder suggests that something is wrong with us. A disorder cannot be cured, only managed. In my experience, such an assertion is not true. Post-traumatic stress is an injury, something requiring healing. If done correctly, healing from mental adversity makes you stronger, more capable, self-aware, and results in the kind of psychological capital that increases mental acuity and wisdom.

This reframing matters. When Rodger was diagnosed with a "disorder," it felt like a permanent label – something broken that would never be fixed, only managed. When he began thinking of it as an "injury," everything changed. Injuries heal. Injuries respond to treatment. Injuries don't define you; they're something that happened to you.

This book, and the associated Navigating Adversity training course, provides you with many of the same therapeutic tools that worked for me. My EMDR experience was one facet of the healing process – an incredible one, certainly – but it is not the only reason I am thriving today. As an overachiever, being mentally competent is not enough for me. Every day of my life is a gift and because I choose to live life to its fullest, I had to honor each dimension of wellness and learn how to pursue resilience spiritually, cognitively, emotionally, physically, socially, professionally, financially, and psychologically.

From Trauma to Purpose

This experience awakened my desire to become an advanced practitioner of mindfulness, meditation, and resiliency. As a California POST master instructor, I now teach these concepts and practices to other first responders. I cultivated my experience into a podcast, HeroTalk.org, where we explore the tough topics and gaps that exist even today in seeking help for trauma recovery. I am a certified life coach who helps people achieve small wins and major successes. From trauma came beauty. From adversity, triumph. I am honored to share my challenges with you as we journey together in the pursuit of resilience.

What Rodger's Story Teaches Us

Rodger's journey from trauma to recovery illustrates several truths that apply to anyone in this profession:

- Severe psychological injury can happen to anyone – Experience, toughness, and competence offer no protection. Rodger was a seasoned investigator, comfortable with chaos, until the moment he wasn't.
- Symptoms can be invisible – even to you – For five years, Rodger's trauma manifested as reckless heroism that was rewarded rather than recognized as a warning sign. The culture celebrated what was destroying him.

- Multiple traumas stack – The brain buries what it can't process, but those buried wounds don't disappear. They accumulate, waiting to be triggered.
- Complete recovery is possible – Rodger isn't "managing" his trauma. He's healed from it. The emotional charge is gone. This is possible for you too.
- Seeking help requires courage – The professional risks were real, and Rodger paid a career price. But he's alive, thriving, and has his family. Some prices are worth paying.
- The stigma is the enemy – Every officer who doubted Rodger after his treatment was wrong. He became more dependable, not less. The stigma that keeps people from seeking help costs lives.

If You Recognized Yourself in This Chapter

- If Rodger's story stirred something in you – if you saw your own reckless behavior, your own buried memories, your own reluctance to seek help – please hear this:
- You are not broken. You are injured. And injuries heal.
- The resources at the end of this book can help you find a provider who understands first responder culture. The tools in the chapters ahead can begin the healing process. You don't have to hit a breaking point like Rodger did. You can start now

Chapter Four Reflection

These questions are for you alone. Be honest with yourself.

- Have you experienced a critical incident that you haven't fully processed?
- Are there incidents from earlier in your career that you've "buried" and rarely think about?
- Have your risk-taking behaviors changed since entering this profession? How?
- If you needed psychological help, what would prevent you from seeking it?
- Who in your life would you trust enough to tell if you were struggling?
- What would it take for you to believe that seeking help is a sign of strength rather than weakness?

Chapter Five

Cognitive Flexibility: The Epicenter of Resilience Command

Adversity: Post-Traumatic Stress Injury

In the last chapter, you walked through Rodger's journey from a routine call to a catastrophic psychological injury – and ultimately, to complete recovery. His story illustrates something essential about the brain: it can be wounded by what it experiences, but it can also heal. More than that, it can be strengthened to better handle future adversity.

This chapter is about taking command of the very organ that processes every experience you have. Your brain isn't just along for the ride – it's the control center that determines how you respond to danger, how you recover from trauma, and how resilient you become over time. The good news is that you're not at its mercy. With the right understanding and the right tools, your brain becomes an asset you can deliberately develop.

But first, we need to understand what we're defending against.

Understanding Post-Traumatic Stress Injury

One of the most damaging misconceptions about post-traumatic stress is that symptoms appear immediately after a traumatic event. While this can happen, it's far from universal. For survivors of childhood trauma – and research suggests that a significant percentage of first responders fall into this category – PTSI can remain buried for decades, only to be triggered by something in adulthood.

Think about what this means for your profession. The very work you've chosen – rescuing children from harm, responding to domestic violence, witnessing the aftermath of accidents – can unlock memories from your own past that you may not even consciously remember. Being triggered as an adult adds a complex layer to an already demanding job. Long-forgotten memories surface, making it difficult to concentrate. Old wounds reopen, leaving you feeling vulnerable, confused, and frightened.

Without understanding what's happening, the natural response is to reach for something – anything – that numbs the pain. But numbing doesn't heal. It just delays the reckoning.

The Prevalence You Don't Hear About

Current research paints a sobering picture of PTSI rates across first responder professions:

- Law enforcement: 6-32% experience PTSI symptoms
- EMT/Paramedics: 9-22%
- Firefighters: 17-32%
- 911 Dispatchers: Studies suggest rates comparable to field responders

But these numbers only capture those with diagnosable symptoms. The more common reality is what researchers call chronic, sub-threshold PTSI – symptoms mild enough that people learn to live with them, adjusting their daily lives around the edges. They avoid certain streets, startle at unexpected sounds, struggle with sleep, but never seek help because the symptoms don't feel "bad enough."

An estimated 50% of first responders are living with some form of chronic stress injury. Of those with more severe symptoms, only about 10% seek diagnosis and treatment.

FIELD PERSPECTIVE

"For years I thought everyone felt the way I did – always on edge, never quite able to relax, replaying calls in my head at 3 AM. It wasn't until I finally talked to someone that I realized what I was living with wasn't normal. It was treatable."

– Paramedic, 12 years of service

The Types of PTSI

Chronic PTSI is the most common form in first response. The symptoms are persistent but mild – frequent enough that you adapt to them, severe enough that they diminish your quality of life. Because they rarely reach clinical threshold, most people living with chronic PTSI never receive treatment.

Acute PTSI emerges after a specific traumatic event and involves more pronounced symptoms: intrusive memories, significant avoidance behaviors, hypervigilance, and emotional numbing. This is what most people picture when they think of trauma – but it's not the only form.

Complex PTSI (C-PTSI) develops when trauma isn't a single event but an accumulation – wound upon wound in the same place. As you read in Rodger's story, he didn't just experience one critical incident; EMDR therapy revealed six additional buried traumas. If you visualize acute PTSI as a puncture wound, complex PTSI is the much larger hole left by multiple injuries to the same tissue.

Symptoms of Post-Traumatic Stress Injury

> According to the National Institute of Mental Health, PTSI symptoms fall into four categories:
>
> Re-experiencing: Flashbacks, intrusive memories, distressing dreams, physical stress responses to reminders
>
> Avoidance: Staying away from places, events, or objects that trigger memories; avoiding thoughts or feelings related to the trauma
>
> Arousal: Hypervigilance, being easily startled, feeling tense or 'on edge,' difficulty sleeping, irritability, engaging in risky or destructive behaviors
>
> Cognition/Mood: Trouble remembering key elements of the event, negative thoughts about yourself or the world, distorted feelings of guilt or blame, loss of interest in enjoyable activities, difficulty feeling positive emotions
>
> The more symptoms present, and the more frequently they occur, the more severe the injury

A Critical Distinction

Some of these symptoms – particularly loss of interest, emotional numbness, negative thinking, and risk-taking behavior – also appear in conditions that aren't trauma-based. Research distinguishes between PTSI (rooted in specific traumatic exposure) and conditions like apathy (feeling nothing, distinct from depression), boredom-driven anhedonia (loss of interest due to understimulation rather than trauma), and person-environment mismatch (chronic tension from work that doesn't fit your wiring).

The key diagnostic question: Can you trace your symptoms to a specific incident or accumulation of traumatic exposures? If yes, PTSI treatment is likely appropriate. If your symptoms emerged gradually without clear traumatic origin – or if they lift temporarily when you're engaged in meaningful challenge – the root cause may be organizational rather than traumatic, and the interventions differ accordingly.

Treatment That Works

If you're recognizing yourself in these descriptions, here's the most important thing to know: effective treatment exists. PTSI is not a life sentence.

Eye Movement Desensitization and Reprocessing (EMDR) remains the gold standard for trauma treatment. It's the therapy that transformed Rodger's life – allowing him to recall traumatic events with clarity but without the overwhelming emotional charge. EMDR works by helping the brain properly process and store traumatic memories, reducing their power to trigger present-moment distress.

Cognitive Processing Therapy (CPT) helps you examine and reframe the beliefs that developed because of trauma – the "I should have done more" or "I can't trust anyone" thoughts that become embedded after critical incidents.

Prolonged Exposure Therapy gradually and safely exposes you to trauma-related memories, feelings, and situations you've been avoiding, reducing their power over time.

Emerging modalities are showing promise as well. Virtual reality-augmented exposure therapy is being piloted specifically for first responder PTSI, allowing clinicians to recreate scenarios in controlled environments. While still experimental, early results are encouraging.

Finding The Right Provider

> Research consistently emphasizes the importance of working with providers who understand first responder culture. A 2024 study in Psychological Services specifically noted that effective treatment requires clinicians trained to understand emotional detachment as a coping mechanism, rigid cognitive styles that develop from the job, and preferences toward structure and action.
>
> A therapist who doesn't understand why you can't 'just talk about your feelings' or who judges your dark humor isn't going to help you. Look for providers who specialize in first responders, military, or other high-stress professions. The resources section at the end of this book can help you start that search.

We cross our bridges when we come to them and burn them behind us, with nothing to show for our progress except a memory of the smell of smoke, and a presumption that once our eyes watered.

– **Sir Tom Stoppard**

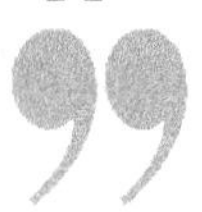

Your Brain: The Control Center

To build cognitive resilience, you first need to understand how the brain works – not at a PhD level, but enough to recognize what's happening inside your head during both normal operations and crisis.

Think of your brain as having four key players that work together whenever you encounter anything significant:

The Amygdala: Your Alarm System

You have two small, almond-shaped structures – one on each side of your brain – that serve as your early warning system. The amygdala's job is to detect threats and trigger protective responses. When something dangerous (or potentially dangerous) happens, the amygdala sounds the alarm.

Here's what makes the amygdala both powerful and problematic: it learns from experience. The more emotionally arousing an event, the more deeply it gets encoded. Every sensory detail from a traumatic incident – the sounds, smells, visual images – gets tagged as potential danger signals.

Consider this example: You're driving past a movie theater and smell fresh popcorn. At that moment, you witness a serious accident. Your brain doesn't just record the accident – it records the smell of popcorn as a warning signal. Unless you consciously process and correct this association, your amygdala may trigger a stress response every time you smell popcorn for the rest of your life.

This is what therapists mean when they talk about "processing" trauma. They're helping you untangle the associations your amygdala made during crisis – separating actual danger from incidental sensory details that happened to be present.

The Hypothalamus: Your Chemical Factory

Once the amygdala sounds the alarm, the hypothalamus responds by flooding your body with the chemicals it thinks you need. Adrenaline for immediate energy. Cortisol for sustained alertness. Norepinephrine for focus.

In a healthy system, these chemicals surge during danger and then clear once the threat passes. The problem is that the hypothalamus takes its cues from the amygdala – and if your amygdala has been conditioned to see danger everywhere, your hypothalamus keeps pumping out stress chemicals even when you're objectively safe.

This is the biological mechanism behind chronic stress. Your chemical factory is running overtime, depleting resources and causing downstream damage to multiple body systems.

The Hippocampus: Your Memory Center

The hippocampus is responsible for forming and retrieving memories. It works closely with the amygdala, but with a crucial difference: while the amygdala tags experiences with emotional significance, the hippocampus provides context – when something happened, where you were, what led up to it.

In PTSI, this relationship gets disrupted. Brain scans of people with chronic stress injuries show that the hippocampus actually shrinks over time, impaired by the constant flood of cortisol. The result? Memories lose their context. A flashback isn't just remembering something bad – it's your brain failing to distinguish between past and present, between memory and current reality.

This is exactly what Rodger experienced during his deposition. When he saw those photographs, his hippocampus couldn't maintain the boundary between "remembering an event from five years ago" and "this is happening right now." His brain transported him back to the scene, complete with smells, sounds, and the overwhelming confusion of that day.

The Frontal Lobe: Your Decision Maker

Your frontal lobe is responsible for executive function – the ability to weigh options, consider consequences, and make deliberate choices rather than reactive ones. It's what separates strategic thinking from pure instinct.

Here's the challenge: under extreme stress, the brain can bypass the frontal lobe entirely. When the amygdala perceives immediate danger, it can trigger the hypothalamus directly, flooding your body with chemicals before your frontal lobe has a chance to evaluate whether the threat is real.

In Rodger's case, his post-traumatic stress injury essentially put a "DO NOT ENTER" sign in front of his hippocampus and frontal lobe. His behavior after the critical incident – the reckless heroism, the danger-seeking – happened without the benefit of either memory context or consequence evaluation. He was operating on raw amygdala-hypothalamus circuitry.

RODGER'S REFLECTION

Understanding the brain science was a turning point for me. I'd spent years thinking I was weak, broken, or crazy. Learning that my brain was doing exactly what it was designed to do – protecting me from

perceived threats – helped me stop blaming myself and start working with my biology instead of against it

The OODA Loop: Training Your Brain for Crisis

Now that you understand how the brain processes threat, let's talk about how to train it for better performance under pressure. One of the most powerful tools for building mental agility comes from an unexpected source: a fighter pilot.

John Boyd was a military strategist who revolutionized how we think about decision-making in high-stakes situations. His framework – the OODA Loop – has been adopted by everyone from Navy SEALs to emergency responders to business executives. It stands for Observe, Orient, Decide, Act.

The genius of the OODA Loop isn't just that it describes how decisions get made – it reveals how you can make them better and faster by deliberately training each step.

Observe

The first step is taking in information about what's happening. This sounds obvious, but it's where most people go wrong. Under stress, we tend to:

- Rush to assumption, blocking out information that doesn't fit what we expect
- Let emotions color what we perceive
- See what we're looking for rather than what's there

Consider the dispatcher who receives a call from the same address for the fifth time this month – another domestic disturbance at a home where the victim never presses charges. The temptation is to make assumptions based on past calls. But those assumptions can be deadly. Today might be different. Today the abuser might have a weapon. Today the caller might be someone else entirely.

True observation requires deliberately suspending judgment long enough to collect actual data. It fights against the brain's natural tendency to fill in gaps with assumptions.

Orient

This is the most important step – and the one most people skip. Orientation is about making sense of what you've observed by breaking apart your assumptions and rebuilding your understanding based on current reality.

Boyd called this "destructive deduction" – pulling apart what you think you know – followed by "creative induction" – forming new mental pathways that align with what's in front of you.

Here's an exercise Boyd used in his workshops. Read it slowly and let each image form in your mind:

Imagine you're on a ski slope with other skiers. Now imagine you're in Florida, riding in an outboard motorboat. Next, picture yourself riding a bicycle on a spring day. Finally, imagine you're in a department store, watching a child fascinated by toy tractors with rubber treads.

Now: mentally remove the skis from the slope. Take the outboard motor from the boat. Remove the handlebars from the bicycle. Take the rubber treads from the toy tractor.

You now have skis, an outboard motor, handlebars, and rubber treads. What can you build?

If you saw a snowmobile, you've just practiced orientation – taking disparate elements and synthesizing them into something new that fits current reality.

Boyd said: "A loser is someone who cannot build snowmobiles when facing uncertainty. A winner is someone who can build snowmobiles, and employ them appropriately, when facing unpredictable change."

Every time you practice this kind of thinking – breaking apart assumptions and rebuilding understanding – you create new neural pathways. The more pathways you have, the faster you can orient when reality doesn't match expectations.

Decide

Once you've observed and oriented, decision becomes relatively straightforward – you're choosing among the options your orientation generated. The key insight here is that you're never working with perfect information. The decision you make won't be perfect. It will be "good enough for right now."

This matters because perfectionism is the enemy of action. Waiting for certainty in uncertain situations gets people killed.

Act

Action is the test. You find out immediately whether your observation, orientation, and decision were accurate. If they were, you win. If not, you immediately cycle back through the loop with new information.

The power of the OODA Loop isn't in getting it right the first time – it's in cycling through faster than your adversary or faster than the situation is changing. Boyd said: "If your opponent can cycle through the loop faster than you, your own actions become outdated and disconnected from true reality, and your opponent's advantage increases geometrically."

For first responders, the "opponent" is often the situation itself – a crisis that's evolving faster than you can respond. The more mental pathways you've built through practice, the faster you can orient and act.

> **FIELD PERSPECTIVE**
> *"I run scenarios in my head constantly – on the drive to work, during slow moments, before sleep. What if a shooter enters here? What if that car runs the light? What if this call isn't what it sounds like? My wife thinks I'm paranoid. I call it mental preparation. The day I stopped being surprised by chaos was the day I started being effective in it."*
>
> ***– SWAT Officer, 14 years of service***

Collaborating with Your Brain

The OODA Loop trains your brain for external challenges. But there's another dimension to cognitive resilience: learning to work with your brain's natural tendencies rather than against them.

Marisa Peer, a psychologist who works with Olympic athletes, has identified four principles that govern how the brain operates. Understanding these gives you leverage points for change.

Your Brain Wants to Give You What You Want

Your brain is constantly listening to what you say – out loud and silently – and interpreting it as instructions. When you tell yourself (or others) "This project is impossible; I'll never finish; I wish I could just call in sick," your brain hears: "This is something to be avoided." It will helpfully generate obstacles – headaches, fatigue, illness – to give you what it thinks you want.

The inverse is equally powerful. When you connect difficult tasks to meaningful outcomes – "This gets me closer to what I really want" – your brain shifts from resistance to support.

This isn't positive thinking for its own sake. It's understanding that your brain treats your words as commands and then delivers accordingly.

Your Brain Loves What It Knows

When facing new situations, your brain searches its existing mental pathways for relevant experience. If it can't find direct experience, it draws on secondhand sources – what you've heard, read, or seen in media.

This is where bias originates. Your brain makes instant assumptions about people and situations based on past encounters. In a profession where you're regularly exposed to the 5% of the population doing the most harm, the natural tendency is to project those experiences onto the other 95%.

The antidote is deliberately seeking new knowledge and experiences. This is particularly important for the four percent. Research on sensation-seeking shows that people drawn to high-stakes professions have neurobiological differences in how they process stimulation – they require more novelty and challenge to feel engaged. When your brain "loves what it knows," but what it knows is high-intensity work, routine assignments can feel like deprivation rather than relief. Understanding this wiring helps you distinguish between genuine recovery needs and the understimulation that masquerades as burnout. Expose yourself to cultures, perspectives, and people outside your usual orbit. Replace assumption-based pathways with knowledge-based ones.

Your Brain Responds to Images and Words

You receive between three and five thousand messages every day – from media, advertising, conversations, and your own internal dialogue. Each one influences what your brain believes is possible, desirable, and true.

Taking control of this input is one of the most powerful things you can do for your mental health. What you watch. What you read. What you scroll through. What you tell yourself when no one's listening. All of it is programming your brain.

The first responder who spends off-hours consuming violent media, doomscrolling news feeds, and mentally rehearsing everything that could go wrong is training their brain for anxiety. The one who deliberately inputs messages of capability, calm, and purpose is training for resilience.

Your Brain Seeks Pleasure and Avoids Pain

This is the most fundamental program running in your brain. It will always move you toward what feels good and away from what feels bad – unless you deliberately override it.

The override comes through linking. Marathon runners don't naturally enjoy the pain of training. They've learned to link short-term discomfort to the long-term pleasure of accomplishment, fitness, and identity as a runner. Eventually, the discomfort itself becomes associated with pleasure.

You can do this with any difficult task. Instead of dreading the hard work of recovery, therapy, or self-improvement, link it to what you want: a longer career, better relationships, peace of mind, the chance to meet your grandchildren.

The Breathwork Connection

Before we move to activities, it's essential to understand how breath connects to cognitive function. In Chapter Two, you learned breathwork techniques for physical recovery. Here, we're using breath specifically for mental performance.

When you're stressed, breathing becomes shallow and rapid – which signals to your brain that danger is present, which releases more stress chemicals, which makes breathing even more shallow. It's a feedback loop that keeps you locked in fight-or-flight.

Deliberate breathing breaks this loop. By consciously slowing and deepening your breath, you send a clear signal to your nervous system: "The danger has passed. It's safe to think clearly now."

Navy SEALs and elite athletes use this connection deliberately. Before high-stakes situations, they engage breathing techniques paired with mental visualization to build neural pathways. They're literally training their brains to perform under conditions that would paralyze an untrained mind.

Cognitive Reset Breath

Use this before making important decisions or when you feel mental fog descending.

1. Inhale through your nose for 4 counts

2. Hold for 4 counts

3. Exhale through your mouth for 4 counts

4. Hold empty for 4 counts

Repeat 4 times. During the exhales, visualize mental clutter being expelled. During the inhales, visualize clarity entering.

This technique shifts your nervous system from reactive to receptive, priming your brain for better decision-making.

Activities for Building Cognitive Capital

Research shows that consistent practice of these activities for at least six weeks can refire atrophied neural connections and build new pathways. These aren't one-time exercises – they're habits to incorporate into your life.

When you experience the symptoms described in this chapter, can you trace them to specific traumatic exposures – or did they emerge gradually as your work became more routine, bureaucratic, or misaligned with what drew you to this profession? Your answer points toward different intervention pathways.

5-Minute Quick Wins

Start here. These require no equipment or special preparation.

Mental Snapshot: Wherever you are right now, close your eyes. How many exits are there? Where are the potential threats? What resources are available if something goes wrong? Open your eyes and check your accuracy. Do this several times daily – it builds observation skills while you go about normal life.

Assumption Check: The next time you make a quick judgment about a person or situation, pause. Ask yourself: What am I assuming? What do I know? Is there another explanation? This takes 30 seconds and trains your brain to separate observation from interpretation.

Cognitive Reset Breath: Before responding to a stressful email, having a difficult conversation, or making any significant decision: stop. Do two minutes of box breathing (4-4-4-4). Notice how your thinking changes.

Reframe Practice: When you catch yourself saying something negative ("This is impossible"), immediately restate it in a way that gives your brain useful instructions ("This is challenging, and solving it will prove what I'm capable of").

15-Minute-Deep Practice

For when you can be uninterrupted.

Scenario Building: Choose a location you spend time in – your home, your workplace, a restaurant you frequent. Spend 15 minutes mentally rehearsing different emergency scenarios. What would you do if X happened? What about Y? Where would you go? What resources would you use? Write down at least three scenarios with specific response plans.

Input Audit: Review what you've consumed in the past 24 hours – news, social media, entertainment, conversations. How much of it fed anxiety, negativity, or distraction? How much supported calm, capability, or growth? Make one specific change for tomorrow.

Trigger Mapping: Identify something that consistently triggers a stress response in you – a sound, smell, person, or situation. Write down exactly what the trigger is, what physical sensations arise, what thoughts follow, and what behavior typically results. Understanding the chain gives you intervention points.

Heart Coherence Practice: Sit comfortably with feet flat on the ground. Visualize someone you love deeply. Breathe slowly through your nose, imagining the breath flowing directly into your heart. With each breath, expand the feeling of love. Continue for 10-15 minutes. Research shows this practice can provide nervous system benefits for up to six hours.

30-Minute Full Engagement

For your dedicated cognitive training time.

Uniform Ritual Development: Create a deliberate pre-shift and post-shift mental transition. Before work: use getting dressed as a visualization exercise – each piece of uniform represents a capability you're putting on (alertness, competence, resilience). After work: use the drive home for mental processing (jamming music, talking through the day). At home, removing the uniform becomes a symbolic release of vigilance. Practice this complete ritual, noting how it affects your mental state.

Brain Fuel Experiment: Day 1: Eat your normal diet and log how you feel after each meal – energy, clarity, mood. Day 2: Fuel your brain deliberately (salmon, avocados, nuts, dark leafy greens, adequate water). Log the same measures. Day 3: Compare. Most people are shocked by the difference. Your brain uses 20% of your calories; what you feed it matters.

Wim Hof Inspired Practice: Spend 10 minutes on deliberate breathing to prepare your neurological system for the day. Then, gradually introduce controlled discomfort – starting with cooler showers and progressing to cold. This trains your brain to remain calm when conditions aren't comfortable, building tolerance for ambiguity and stress.

4-7-8 Meditation: Sit comfortably. Inhale for 4 counts. Hold for 7 counts. Exhale for 8 counts. No hold after exhale – immediately begin the next breath. During each phase, repeat a positive affirmation ("I am calm and focused," "My thinking is clear," "I respond rather than react"). Continue for 20-30 minutes. Note: 20 minutes of this practice can replace up to 90 minutes of sleep in terms of recovery benefit.

Resource Recommendations

For guided meditation and breathwork, several apps offer first responder discounts or free tiers:

- Headspace (headspace.com) - First responder discount available
- Insight Timer - Free, with thousands of guided practices
- Calm - 7-day free trial, variety of programs
- Responder Strong - Designed specifically for first responders

For deeper learning on cognitive training, consider taking an online course outside your field – history, philosophy, art, science. Building mental pathways through diverse learning directly improves cognitive flexibility.

Chapter Five Reflection

Consider these questions honestly. Your answers are for you alone.

- Do you recognize any symptoms of PTSI in yourself? Which category (re-experiencing, avoidance, arousal, cognition/mood)?
- When was the last time you were genuinely surprised by a situation at work? What does that tell you about your observation skills?
- What assumptions do you make repeatedly that might limit your effectiveness?
- What messages are you feeding your brain daily? Are they serving you?
- What one cognitive practice from this chapter will you commit to for the next six weeks?

Chapter Six

Emotional Self Regulation & Mastery

Adversity: Anxiety

You're lying in bed after a difficult shift. Physically exhausted, but your mind won't stop. You replay conversations, second-guess decisions, rehearse tomorrow's challenges. Your heart rate refuses to slow down. Sleep feels impossible – and the harder you try to relax, the more wound up you become.

Or maybe it's subtler than that. A constant low-grade tension you've learned to live with. Irritability that flares at minor frustrations. A sense that something bad is about to happen, even when everything is objectively fine. You've adjusted your life around these feelings without ever naming them for what they are.

Anxiety is one of the most common adversities first responders face, and one of the most frequently dismissed. It presents itself in so many forms – some dramatic, some easy to ignore – that many people live with it for years without recognizing it as something that can be addressed.

Recognizing Anxiety

Anxiety symptoms exist on a spectrum, and the early warning signs are often mistaken for normal stress:

- Persistent irritability that seems disproportionate to triggers
- Restlessness – difficulty sitting still or feeling comfortable
- A vague sense of impending doom or dread
- Trouble concentrating or following through on tasks
- Physical tension – clenched jaw, tight shoulders, stomach issues
- Increased heart rate and rapid breathing, even at rest
- Excessive worry that feels impossible to control
- Sleep disruption – trouble falling asleep, staying asleep, or waking rested

When these symptoms go unaddressed, they can escalate. What starts as general anxiety can develop into panic attacks – sudden, overwhelming episodes of fear accompanied by physical symptoms like chest pain, shortness of breath, and a sense of losing control. Ongoing anxiety can crystallize into specific phobias or social anxiety disorder.

And here's the dangerous pattern: anxiety is deeply uncomfortable, so the natural response is to reach for something that provides relief. Alcohol to quiet the mind. Sleep medication to force rest. Adrenaline-seeking behaviors to override the discomfort with a more familiar feeling. Temporary relief reinforces the behavior, creating a cycle that can lead to substance dependence on top of the underlying anxiety.

When Restlessness Isn't Anxiety

Some of these symptoms – particularly restlessness, difficulty concentrating, and the urge toward high-intensity activity – can indicate something other than anxiety. Research on sensation-seeking shows that people wired for high-stakes work (the four percent) have neurobiological differences in how they process stimulation. When their environment fails to provide adequate challenge, they experience what researchers call "understimulation distress" – a restless, uncomfortable state that looks identical to anxiety but has opposite causes.

The diagnostic question: Does your restlessness increase when life gets *more* demanding, or when it gets *less* demanding? True anxiety escalates with increased pressure. Understimulation distress escalates with routine, boredom, and lack of meaningful challenge. The interventions differ accordingly – anxiety benefits from calming practices, while understimulation requires increased engagement with meaningful work.

FIELD PERSPECTIVE

"I didn't realize I had anxiety for fifteen years. I just thought I was 'intense' or 'wired differently.' It wasn't until my wife pointed out that normal people don't check the locks five times or lie awake planning for disasters that might never happen. Once I had a name for it, I could actually do something about it."

– Detective, 18 years of service

He who controls others may be powerful, but he who has mastered himself is mightier still.

– Lao Tzu

The Two Systems That Govern Your Emotional Life

To master your emotional responses, you need to understand the two systems that produce them. Think of them as the gas pedal and brake pedal of your nervous system.

The Sympathetic Nervous System: Your Accelerator

When you perceive danger – or anything your brain interprets as a threat – your sympathetic nervous system (SNS) activates. This is your body's accelerator pedal, and when it's pressed, everything speeds up:

- Heart rate increases to pump blood to large muscle groups
- Breathing quickens to bring in more oxygen
- Pupils dilate to take in more visual information
- Digestion stops – there's no time for that now
- Sweat glands open to cool the body for action
- Tunnel vision narrows your focus to the perceived threat

Simultaneously, your brain triggers the release of adrenaline and cortisol – the chemical fuel for whatever action you're about to take. In a genuine emergency, this system is lifesaving. It's what allows you to perform under conditions that would paralyze others.

The problem is that this system can't distinguish between a real threat and a perceived one. A tense email from your supervisor triggers the same cascade as an armed suspect. An argument with your spouse activates the same chemistry as a critical incident. And for first responders who've experienced trauma, the threshold for activation gets lower over time. You start living with your foot on the accelerator.

The Parasympathetic Nervous System: Your Brake

Once danger passes, your parasympathetic nervous system (PNS) is supposed to take over. This is your brake pedal – the system that brings you back to baseline:

- Heart rate slows
- Breathing deepens and steadies
- Digestion resumes
- Muscles release tension
- The flood of stress chemicals begins to clear

This process takes time, and it often leaves you feeling drained. That exhaustion after a high-intensity shift isn't weakness – it's your PNS doing its job, bringing your body back into balance. When you come home and feel unable to engage with your family, it's often because your nervous system is still working to return to normal.

Here's the critical insight: the PNS can only do its job if you let it. And for many first responders, that's exactly what doesn't happen.

The Trap of Hormonal Purgatory

The state between full activation (SNS) and full recovery (PNS) is deeply uncomfortable. You're not amped up enough to feel powerful, but you're not relaxed enough to feel peaceful. You're in limbo.

The common response? Do something to get that activated feeling back. Seek out conflict. Make risky choices. Have another drink. Scroll through content that triggers outrage. Anything to escape the discomfort of the in-between.

This is how people get stuck – never fully recovering before the next activation, burning through their reserves, making decisions from a place of chronic dysregulation.

Breaking this cycle requires deliberately supporting your PNS through activities that feel foreign at first: breathwork, meditation, gentle movement, stillness. It means tolerating the discomfort of recovery instead of bypassing it.

A Note for the 4%

If the "hormonal purgatory" described above feels less like incomplete recovery and more like being trapped in a body that needs to *do something*, pay attention to that signal. Research on sensation-seeking suggests that people wired for high-stakes work have different optimal arousal levels than the general population. What feels like "calm" to others may genuinely feel like deprivation to you.

This doesn't mean you should skip recovery – chronic stress still causes damage. But it does mean your recovery might need to look different: active rather than passive, engaging rather than still. A challenging hike rather than meditation. A complex problem to solve rather than an empty evening. The goal is genuine restoration, not forcing yourself into a recovery template that doesn't fit your wiring.

FIELD PERSPECTIVE

"After hot calls, I used to go straight to the gym and lift heavy. I thought I was 'working off' the stress. What I was doing was keeping my nervous system revved. When I started doing breathwork in my car before going home, my wife noticed the difference before I did. I was actually present instead of just physically there."

– Firefighter/Paramedic, 11 years of service

Breath: Your Direct Line to the Nervous System

Of all the tools for emotional regulation, breath is the most powerful and the most accessible. Here's why: your breath is the only autonomic function that operates both automatically AND under your conscious control. You don't have to think about breathing – but you can choose to change it at any moment.

This gives you a direct line to your nervous system. When you deliberately slow and deepen your breath, you send an unmistakable signal: "The danger has passed. It's safe to recover now." Your heart rate responds. Your muscle tension responds. Your brain chemistry responds.

The first responders who master emotional regulation aren't the ones with iron willpower – they're the ones who've learned to use breath as a reset button.

The Physiological Sigh: Fastest Emotional Reset

When you need to shift your state quickly – before a difficult conversation, after a stressful call, in any moment when emotions are threatening to take over – use the physiological sigh.

1. Take a full breath in through your nose

2. At the top, add a second short inhale (a 'top-off' breath) to fully expand your lungs

3. Release with a long, slow exhale through your mouth – as long as you can comfortably extend it

Research from Stanford shows this is the fastest way to activate the parasympathetic response. One or two cycles can measurably shift your nervous system state.

4-4-4 Box Breathing: Sustained Calm

For longer regulation or preparation before known stressors:

- Inhale through your nose for 4 counts
- Hold for 4 counts (without tensing jaw or shoulders)
- Exhale through your mouth for 4 counts
- Hold empty for 4 counts
- Repeat 4-6 cycles

This pattern tells your brain: 'I am in control. There is no emergency.' Use it before shifts, before difficult conversations, or any time you need to establish baseline calm.

The Power of Emotional Vocabulary

Here's something that might surprise you: the words you use to describe your emotions directly affect your ability to regulate them.

When someone asks how you're doing and you say "Fine" or "Bad," you're taking a hands-off approach to emotional awareness. Your brain receives vague instructions and responds vaguely. But when you can accurately name what you're feeling – "I'm feeling resentful about how that call was handled" or "I'm anxious about the conversation I need to have tomorrow" – you give your brain specific information to work with.

Research shows that the simple act of labeling an emotion reduces its intensity. Neuroscientists call this "affect labeling" – putting feelings into words activates the prefrontal cortex (your thinking brain) and reduces activity in the amygdala (your alarm system). Naming the feeling is itself a regulatory act.

The problem is that most of us have a limited emotional vocabulary. We default to a handful of terms: good, bad, fine, stressed, tired, angry. These are like trying to paint with only three colors – you can get the general idea across, but you miss all the nuance.

Expanding Your Emotional Vocabulary

Psychologist Robert Plutchik identified eight core emotions, each with varying intensities. Learning to distinguish between these gives you far more precision in understanding and regulating your emotional state.

FEAR → APPREHENSION → TERROR Worry, anxiety, nervousness, dread, panic, alarm
ANGER → ANNOYANCE → RAGE Irritation, frustration, hostility, resentment, fury, bitterness
SADNESS → PENSIVENESS → GRIEF Disappointment, loneliness, sorrow, melancholy, despair, anguish
JOY → SERENITY → ECSTASY Contentment, hope, optimism, satisfaction, delight, elation
DISGUST → BOREDOM → LOATHING Dislike, aversion, distaste, revulsion, contempt, detestation

SURPRISE → DISTRACTION → AMAZEMENT
Uncertainty, confusion, astonishment, shock, wonder, disbelief
TRUST → ACCEPTANCE → ADMIRATION
Confidence, faith, respect, appreciation, fondness, devotion
ANTICIPATION → INTEREST → VIGILANCE
Curiosity, expectation, eagerness, alertness, excitement, readiness

Notice how different "I'm angry" feels from "I'm feeling resentful" or "I'm experiencing bitterness." Each word carries different information about the actual emotional state – and different implications for what might help.

Pay particular attention to where you fall on the DISGUST → BOREDOM → LOATHING spectrum. Occasional boredom is normal. But chronic boredom in the four percent isn't just an emotion to regulate – it's diagnostic information. Research confirms that boredom "is not simply a milder form of depression, but represents a distinct state" that, left unaddressed, creates its own cascade of symptoms. If you find yourself frequently experiencing boredom, distaste, or contempt related to your work, the issue may not be emotional regulation – it may be fit.

RODGER'S REFLECTION

On the scene at Stonypoint and Hearn, I couldn't have articulated anything beyond confusion and fear. Today, I can describe that experience with precision: the anticipation turning to dread, the horror of what I thought I saw, the relief mixed with continued alarm, the exhaustion layered with grief. That vocabulary didn't come naturally – I had to build it through practice. But having those words gave me power over experiences that once had power over me.

The Connection Between Thought and Emotion

Emotions don't appear from nowhere. They're generated by your interpretation of events – the meaning you assign to what happens. Two people can experience the same situation and have completely different emotional responses based on how they interpret it.

This is important because it means you're not at the mercy of your circumstances. You can't always control what happens, but you can develop influence over how you interpret and respond to it.

The sequence works like this: Event → Interpretation → Emotion → Behavior. A supervisor gives critical feedback (event). You interpret it as an attack on your competence (interpretation). You feel defensive and resentful (emotion). You become dismissive or argumentative (behavior).

But what if the interpretation changed? Same feedback, but you interpret it as useful information for improvement. Now you might feel curious or motivated instead of defensive. Your behavior shifts accordingly.

This isn't about positive thinking or pretending things don't bother you. It's about recognizing that you have a choice point between stimulus and response – and emotional mastery is the ability to operate from that choice point instead of reacting on autopilot.

The Stoic Question

- When you notice a strong emotional reaction, pause and ask: What interpretation am I making about this situation that's generating this feeling?
- Then ask: Is this interpretation accurate? Is it useful? Is there another way to see this?
- This isn't about suppressing emotions – it's about not being controlled by interpretations you've never examined.

Emotional Regulation in Relationships

First responders often report that their emotional regulation is better at work than at home. This seems paradoxical – shouldn't you be more controlled in high-stakes situations? – but it makes sense when you understand the nervous system.

At work, you're in performance mode. The SNS activation that comes with danger or stress is channeled into action. You have training, protocols, and a clear role. The emotions get used as fuel.

At home, you're supposed to shift into recovery mode. But your PNS may still be working to restore balance. You're depleted. And the people closest to you are the ones around whom you feel safe enough to drop your guard – which means they see what you've been holding together all day.

The result is often that minor frustrations at home trigger disproportionate reactions. You snap at your spouse over something trivial. You're short with your kids. You withdraw into screens or substances rather than connecting.

This pattern damages relationships over time – and the damaged relationships become another source of stress, feeding the cycle.

FIELD PERSPECTIVE

"My wife used to say she never knew which version of me was coming home. I thought I was protecting her by not talking about work, but what I was doing was bringing home all the tension without any of the context. Learning to actually transition – to process before I walk in the door – changed everything."

– Patrol Sergeant, 15 years of service

The Transition Ritual

One of the most effective tools for protecting your relationships is a deliberate transition between work mode and home mode. This isn't about compartmentalizing or pretending work didn't happen – it's about giving your nervous system time to shift states before you walk into a different environment.

Options for transition rituals:

- Use your commute for processing: talk through the day out loud, even if no one's listening
- Sit in your driveway for five minutes doing breathwork before going inside
- Change out of work clothes immediately and shower – a physical transition
- Take a brief walk around the block before entering your home
- Have a consistent greeting ritual with family that marks the shift

The specific ritual matters less than having one. What you're doing is creating a boundary that tells your nervous system: "That context is over. This context is different. It's safe to shift modes."

Activities for Building Emotional Capital

Emotional regulation is a skill that develops with practice. These activities are organized from quick interventions to deeper work.

Does your restlessness increase when demands increase (suggesting anxiety) or when demands decrease (suggesting understimulation)? What does this tell you about what your nervous system needs?

5-Minute Quick Wins

Use these in the moment when emotions threaten to take control.

Physiological Sigh Reset: When you notice your emotional state escalating – anger, anxiety, frustration – stop and do 2-3 physiological sighs (double inhale, long exhale). Don't try to think your way out of the emotion; just change your breath and let your nervous system follow.

Name It to Tame It: When you're feeling 'bad' or 'stressed,' get specific. What exactly are you feeling? Use the emotional vocabulary above. Is it resentment? Apprehension? Disappointment? The act of accurately naming the emotion begins to regulate it.

The Interpretation Check: When you notice a strong emotional reaction, pause and ask: What interpretation am I making? Is it accurate? Is it useful? Is there another way to see this? You don't have to change your interpretation – just examining it creates space between stimulus and response.

Temperature Shift: Splash cold water on your face, hold an ice cube, or step outside into cold air. The sudden temperature change activates the dive reflex, which triggers parasympathetic response. It's a physiological shortcut to calming down.

15-Minute-Deep Practice

For when you can be uninterrupted.

Emotional Trigger Mapping: Think of a recent situation that triggered a strong emotional reaction. In your journal, write: What happened? What did I feel (be specific)? What interpretation was I making? How did I behave as a result? Now trace back – have you had similar reactions before? Is there a pattern? Identifying triggers is the first step to changing your response to them.

Rodger's Story Exercise: Reread Rodger's account of his critical incident (Chapter 3). List every emotion word he uses. Now imagine yourself in a similar situation – what emotions would you likely feel? Write them down using the most specific vocabulary you can. This builds both emotional vocabulary and empathic awareness.

Music Regulation Experiment: Close your eyes and listen to your favorite upbeat song. Notice your emotional state before, during, and after. Then choose a calming instrumental piece and repeat. Research shows that calming music activates the parasympathetic nervous system and even supports immune function. What music could you add to your daily routine for regulation?

Refuel Inventory: List activities that genuinely restore you – not distract you, but leave you feeling better afterward. When did you last do each one? What's preventing you from doing them more regularly? Choose one and schedule it this week.

30-Minute Full Engagement

For dedicated emotional development.

Heart Coherence Practice: Sit comfortably with feet flat on the ground and spine straight. Bring to mind someone you love deeply – a child, partner, parent, or even a pet. Feel the love you have for them as fully as you can. Now breathe slowly through your nose, imagining each breath flowing directly into your heart. With each inhale, feel the breath expand the love. Continue for 20-30 minutes. Research shows this practice can provide nervous system benefits for up to six hours afterward.

Transition Ritual Design: Create a deliberate transition practice for moving between work and home. Write out each step – what you'll do, where, for how long. Consider both the physical elements (changing clothes, showering) and the mental/emotional elements (breathwork, processing). Practice the ritual for a week and note its effects on your home interactions.

Weekly Emotional Review: Set aside 30 minutes at the end of each week. Review the major emotional experiences of the week – both positive and negative. For each, identify: the trigger, your interpretation, the emotion (specifically named), your behavior, and the outcome. Look for patterns. What's working? What needs attention? This builds self-awareness over time.

Stress Response Journal: Over the next week, whenever you notice a stress response (elevated heart rate, tension, irritability), log: the situation, your estimated stress hormone level (1-10), any triggers you can identify, how you responded, and how you felt afterward. At the end of the week, analyze: What patterns emerge? Where do you have control? What would you do differently?

WHEN TO SEEK PROFESSIONAL SUPPORT

Emotional regulation is a skill anyone can develop – but some situations benefit from professional guidance:

- Anxiety that significantly impacts daily functioning or relationships
- Panic attacks or phobias that restrict your life
- Emotional reactions that feel uncontrollable despite your efforts
- Reliance on substances to manage emotional states
- Any symptoms that have persisted for weeks without improvement

A therapist who understands first responder culture can help you develop regulation skills faster and address underlying issues that self-help approaches may not reach.

Chapter Six Reflection

Consider these questions honestly. Your answers are for you alone.

- What anxiety symptoms, if any, do you recognize in yourself?
- How would you describe the current balance between your SNS (accelerator) and PNS (brake)?
- What do you typically do in the uncomfortable space between activation and recovery?
- Using specific emotional vocabulary, how are you feeling right now?
- What transition ritual could you implement between work and home?
- What one practice from this chapter will you commit to for the next week?

Chapter Seven

Spiritual Capital: The Foundation of Purpose

Adversity: Burnout & Loss of Purpose

You're driving to work, and something feels different. Not sick, exactly. Not tired, though you are. It's more like... emptiness. You used to feel something when you put on the uniform – pride, purpose, even excitement. Now it's just routine. Another shift. Another day of the same calls, the same frustrations, the same sense that nothing you do really changes anything.

Someone asks why you got into this work, and you have to think about it. The answer that used to come so easily – to help people, to make a difference, to be part of something meaningful – feels hollow now. You say the words, but they don't land the way they used to. You're not even sure you believe them anymore.

This is what burnout looks like from the inside. Not the dramatic collapse that makes headlines, but the slow erosion of purpose. The gradual disconnection from your "why." The quiet death of something essential that used to make the sacrifice feel worth it.

Death is not the greatest loss in life. The greatest loss is what dies inside us while we live.

– Norman Cousins

When Purpose Fades

The most commonly asked question in online psychological forums is: "Why does my life lack purpose?" For most people, this is a philosophical puzzle they'll wrestle with across decades. For first responders, the question cuts deeper – because you entered this profession with purpose overflowing. You didn't have to search for meaning; meaning found you.

You chose this work because something in you needed to protect, to serve, to stand between the vulnerable and the threats they couldn't face alone. That drive wasn't manufactured by a recruiter or a training academy. It was already there – wired into who you are at the deepest level.

And that's what makes the loss so devastating. You didn't lose something you never had. You lost something that was once the very center of who you are.

The Anatomy of Burnout

Burnout isn't just being tired. It's a specific syndrome that develops when the demands of your work consistently exceed your resources for meeting them – and when the meaning that once sustained you begins to evaporate.

The warning signs often appear gradually:

- Emotional exhaustion – Feeling drained before the shift even starts

- Depersonalization – Treating people as problems to manage rather than humans to serve
- Reduced sense of accomplishment – Feeling like your efforts don't matter
- Cynicism – Expecting the worst from people and systems
- Aimlessness – Going through motions without connecting to why
- Hopelessness – Believing nothing will change, so why try

The tragedy is that these symptoms often intensify in the most dedicated people. The ones who gave the most, cared the deepest, and believed the strongest are the ones who fall the hardest when the reservoir runs dry.

> FIELD PERSPECTIVE
>
> *"I used to be the guy who volunteered for overtime, who showed up early and stayed late. Somewhere around year twelve, I realized I was just showing up. Same uniform, same badge, but the person wearing them had checked out. I couldn't remember the last time I felt like I was making a difference."*
>
> – Patrol Officer, 17 years of service

When Burnout Isn't Burnout

The symptoms above can indicate classic burnout – resources depleted by excessive demand. But emerging research suggests they can also indicate something different: understimulation masquerading as exhaustion.

Consider this: you entered this profession because you're wired for challenge. Research on sensation-seeking shows that people drawn to high-stakes work have neurobiological differences in how they process stimulation – they *require* novelty and meaningful challenge to feel engaged. When work becomes routine, bureaucratic, or stripped of the elements that once made it compelling, the four percent can experience symptoms identical to burnout: exhaustion, cynicism, aimlessness, going through the motions.

The diagnostic question: Are you depleted because you're giving too much, or because you're not being asked to give what you're capable of? The interventions differ dramatically. Classic burnout requires rest and boundary-setting. Understimulation requires increased meaningful challenge – the opposite prescription.

If "self-care" recommendations like reducing workload and taking time off leave you feeling *worse* rather than better, you may be treating the wrong condition.

Compassion Fatigue: The Cost of Caring

Burnout is compounded by something specific to helping professions: compassion fatigue. This isn't weakness – it's the predictable result of repeatedly absorbing the suffering of others while depleting your own reserves.

Every call where you witness trauma, every victim you can't save, every family you have to deliver terrible news to – each one makes a withdrawal from your capacity to care. The brain and body aren't designed for unlimited empathy under unlimited stress. At some point, something has to give.

Compassion fatigue shows up as:

- Emotional numbness – Inability to feel what you used to feel for victims

- Irritability with those who need help – Frustration with the very people you're called to serve
- Intrusive images – Scenes from calls appearing unbidden in your mind
- Avoidance – Dreading certain types of calls or situations
- Secondary traumatic stress – Developing PTSI symptoms from others' trauma

The cruel irony is that the people most susceptible to compassion fatigue are the ones who were most compassionate to begin with. You can't burn out a capacity you never had.

The Disconnection From 'Why'

At the core of both burnout and compassion fatigue is a disconnection from purpose – from the 'why' that once made everything make sense.

When you entered this profession, you didn't need to be convinced the work mattered. You felt it. The meaning was self-evident.

But years of exposure to human suffering, systemic dysfunction, and personal sacrifice without adequate replenishment have severed that connection. You know intellectually why the work matters, but you can't feel it anymore.

For some, the disconnection isn't from giving too much – it's from not being *allowed* to give what they have. When the work that once demanded your best becomes routine, bureaucratic, or constrained by policies that don't trust your judgment, purpose can erode even without traumatic exposure. You didn't lose your "why" to suffering; you lost access to the work that expressed it.

This chapter is about rebuilding that connection – not through motivation or willpower, but through deliberate investment in what we call spiritual capital.

Understanding Spiritual Capital

Before you dismiss this section as religious content that doesn't apply to you, read on. What we're calling "spiritual" has very little to do with religion and everything to do with what makes you human.

All animals eat, sleep, and breathe. They compete for resources and accept their place in the ecosystem. Humans are the only species with hopes, dreams, and a desire to live for something beyond ourselves. This uniquely human capacity – the ability to find meaning, to serve something larger than our own survival – is what Rabbi Cary Friedman calls the "uniquely human spirit."

You have this capacity in abundance. It's why you're in this profession instead of one that's safer, easier, or more lucrative. You are, whether you'd use this language or not, an intensely spiritual person. Everything about what drew you to this work – the sense of duty, the drive to protect, the willingness to sacrifice – comes from this spiritual core.

And this core requires sustenance. Just like your body needs food and your mind needs rest, your spirit needs replenishment. Without it, the very thing that makes you uniquely suited for this work begins to wither.

The FBI's Discovery

In the mid-1990s, the FBI's Behavioral Science Unit was analyzing trends in agent wellness from the 1970s forward. Despite advances in equipment, training, and psychological services, the data showed no improvement in rates of addiction, domestic violence, and suicide among their workforce. Something was missing.

When they consulted experts, the feedback was consistent: spiritual health was being ignored. In an agency bound by separation of church and state, no one had figured out how to address the dimension of wellness that provides the foundation for all others.

Their first attempts were disasters. They brought in clergy who treated the sessions as opportunities to preach and convert. Agents sat through uncomfortable hours of religious instruction that had nothing to do with their actual needs. The approach was abandoned repeatedly.

Then a director from the Behavioral Science Unit heard Rabbi Cary Friedman speak. What struck him was the Rabbi's ability to articulate spiritual truths without religious overtones – and his insight that first responders aren't people who need to find spirituality. They're already among the most intensely spiritual people in society. They just need to recognize it and learn to sustain it.

Rabbi Friedman's work transformed how the FBI – and eventually many other agencies – approached this dimension of wellness. His book, "Spiritual Survival for Law Enforcement," remains a foundational text for first responder chaplains nationwide.

FIELD PERSPECTIVE

"I'm not religious at all, and when they said we were doing 'spiritual wellness' training, I almost walked out. But it wasn't about God or church – it was about understanding why I felt so empty when I used to feel so driven. That reframe changed everything for me."

– Detective, 14 years of service

The Three Accounts of Spiritual Capital

Think of your spiritual wellness as a bank with three accounts. Each needs regular deposits to remain healthy. When all three are well-funded, you feel purpose, meaning, and resilience. When they're depleted, you experience the burnout and aimlessness that brought you to this chapter.

Account One: Connection to Something Greater

The first account holds your belief in something beyond yourself – an anchoring point that gives your work meaning even when outcomes are disappointing.

For people of faith, this is straightforward: belief in God or a Higher Power provides the framework. Your work becomes an expression of divine calling. Suffering makes sense within a larger narrative. Tragedy doesn't invalidate purpose because purpose comes from a source beyond human circumstances.

For those without religious faith, this account is just as essential – but it's funded differently. It holds your commitment to an external value system: principles that exist independent of your feelings about them, that would be true whether you believed in them or not.

Examples include the Constitution, the Universal Declaration of Human Rights, the principles encoded in your department's oath of office, or a personal code of ethics you've deliberately adopted. ***The key is that these values are absolute*** – not subject to mood, convenience, or circumstance, ***and external*** - not driven by internal human desires or motivations. They provide a fixed point when everything else feels unstable.

When this account is depleted, you lose your anchor. You start wondering if any of this matters. You question whether the rules you've followed have any validity. Without something to believe in, the sacrifices feel pointless.

Account Two: Belief in People

The second account holds your regard for humanity – your belief that people are worth serving, protecting, and sacrificing for.

You entered this profession because you believed in people. You wanted to protect the innocent, defend the vulnerable, and stand against those who would harm them. That belief was fuel for the hard days.

But your work exposes you to the worst of human behavior. Day after day, you encounter the 5% of the population responsible for 90% of the harm. Predators. Abusers. People who hurt children. People who destroy families. People who take without remorse and never face consequences.

Over time, without deliberate intervention, you start generalizing from the worst to the whole. Everyone becomes suspect. Trust evaporates. Cynicism replaces belief. You protect and serve people you no longer believe deserve it – and that disconnect corrodes everything.

When this account is depleted, you stop seeing the people you serve as fully human. They become problems to manage, cases to close, calls to clear. The compassion that once drove you becomes a liability you can't afford.

Account Three: Confidence in Yourself

The third account holds your belief that you can make a difference – that your effort matters, that your skills are adequate, that your presence changes outcomes for the better.

When you were new, this account was funded by mastery. Every skill you developed, every challenge you overcame, every moment when your training saved someone or solved something – each one deposited confidence into this account.

But time and exposure take their toll. The cases you couldn't solve. The people you couldn't save. The systemic dysfunction that undermined your best efforts. The times you were penalized for doing the right thing or rewarded for the wrong thing. Each one makes a withdrawal.

Add physical or psychological injury, organizational betrayal, or personal failures, and the account can drain rapidly. You start believing you've lost your edge. That you're no longer effective. That it doesn't matter what you do because nothing changes anyway.

When this account is depleted, you stop trying. Why invest effort when effort doesn't pay off? You do the minimum required to keep your job and protect your pension, but the drive for excellence – the hunger to be better – is gone.

The Hidden Drain: Being Unseen

There's a withdrawal pattern that doesn't fit neatly into these three accounts but affects all of them: the experience of being treated generically rather than seen for who you are.

When recognition falls flat because it's delivered in a way that doesn't resonate with you... when trust ruptures go unrepaired because no one knows how to apologize in a way you can receive... when your work assignments don't match your wiring... these experiences drain spiritual capital even when the work itself is meaningful.

If you find your accounts depleting despite doing work you believe in, consider whether the issue is how you're being *treated* rather than what you're being asked to *do*. Sometimes the path to spiritual restoration runs through being genuinely seen – or finding environments where that's possible.

Spiritual States: Where Are You?

> ABUNDANCE – All three accounts are funded. You feel connected to purpose, believe in the people you serve, and trust your ability to make a difference. Challenges feel manageable because you have reserves to draw from.
>
> OVERDRAFT – You've been giving more than you've been receiving. The accounts are low, and you're operating on borrowed spiritual capital. Cynicism is creeping in. Purpose feels distant. You're getting by, but there's no margin.
>
> BANKRUPTCY – The accounts are empty. You've lost connection to your 'why,' stopped believing in people, and doubt your own ability to matter. This is where hopelessness lives. This is where people consider leaving the profession – or worse.
>
> The critical insight: arriving in overdraft or bankruptcy isn't a sign you did something wrong. It usually means you did everything right – gave fully, cared deeply, served sacrificially – without learning to replenish what you were spending.

Reconnecting to Your Why

The path back from burnout isn't about working harder or caring more. It's about deliberately rebuilding what's been depleted. This requires a different kind of effort – not the external effort of doing your job, but the internal effort of tending to your spiritual core.

For first responders, the traditional self-help advice about "finding your purpose" often falls flat. You're not someone who needs to discover meaning – you had it and lost it. The task isn't finding; it's reconnecting.

The Resilience Why

Your "why" may have evolved since you started. That's not a problem – it's growth. The idealistic reasons that drew you to the academy might not be the mature reasons that sustain you now. And that's okay.

What matters is having a why that's current, authentic, and anchored deeply enough to withstand the realities of the work. Not a bumper sticker or a social media bio, but something you believe when no one's watching and the shift has been brutal.

For some, the why connects to faith – a sense of divine calling that transcends daily circumstances. For others, it's commitment to a principle – justice, protection of the vulnerable, the rule of law. For still others, it's personal – providing for family, honoring someone who inspired them, proving something to themselves.

There's no wrong answer. There's only the question: What is your why, right now, today? And is it strong enough to sustain you?

Centering Breath for Purpose

When you feel disconnected from your why – going through motions without meaning – use this practice to reconnect.

1. Find a quiet moment (even 2 minutes in your vehicle)
2. Close your eyes and take three slow, deep breaths
3. On the fourth breath, as you inhale, silently ask: 'Why am I here?'
4. As you exhale, let whatever answer arises come without judgment
5. Repeat for several breaths, letting the question deepen

This isn't about finding the 'right' answer. It's about creating space for your authentic why to surface – even if it's different from what you expected.

The Transition Ritual: Protecting What Matters

One of the most effective tools for maintaining spiritual health is a deliberate transition practice – rituals that mark the boundary between your professional role and the rest of your life.

Before Shift: Armoring Up

Many first responders have an unconscious ritual when putting on the uniform – a mental shift that prepares them for what's ahead. Making this ritual conscious and intentional increases its power.

As you dress for work, treat each item as a deliberate choice. The uniform isn't just clothing – it's a symbol of the values you're choosing to embody. The badge isn't metal – it's a commitment to the people you'll serve today.

A word of caution about self-talk during this transition: what you tell yourself matters. If you armor up with "Everyone's trying to kill me today," your brain will be primed for threat and struggle to de-escalate even with non-threatening citizens. A small adjustment – "I'm prepared for whatever today brings" – keeps you alert without defaulting to hypervigilance.

After Shift: Coming Home

The transition home is even more critical. Your family doesn't need (or deserve) to receive the vigilant, guarded, depleted version of you that just finished a high-stress shift. They need you to arrive – really arrive – present and available.

Options for post-shift transition:

- Commute decompression: Use drive time for processing – talk through the day, listen to music that shifts your state, consciously leave work behind

- Arrival ritual: Sit in the driveway for 5 minutes doing breathwork before going inside
- Physical transition: Change out of uniform immediately, shower, put on comfortable clothes – let the physical change signal the mental shift

Gratitude pivot: Before entering your home, name three things you're grateful for that have nothing to do with work

What you tell yourself during this transition matters too: "I am home. I am safe. I am with people who love me. I can let my guard down here."

FIELD PERSPECTIVE

"I started doing ten minutes of meditation in my car before I go inside. My kids used to scatter when I came home – they could feel the tension radiating off me. Now they run to meet me at the door. That ten minutes is the best investment I make all day."

– Sergeant, 13 years of service

Activities for Building Spiritual Capital

Rebuilding spiritual capital isn't a one-time event – it's an ongoing practice. These activities are organized by which account they replenish.

Are you exhausted because you're giving too much, or because you're not being asked to give what you're capable of? Does the idea of "rest and recovery" feel restorative, or does it feel like more of the emptiness you're already experiencing?

5-Minute Quick Wins

Small deposits that compound over time.

Purpose Touchstone (Account 1): Keep a card in your wallet or on your phone with your 'why' written on it – a sentence or phrase that captures why this work matters to you. Read it once per shift, especially on hard days.

Civilian Appreciation (Account 2): During each shift, deliberately notice one person who represents the good in humanity – someone going about their life with decency, kindness, or integrity. Let them remind you who you're serving.

Win Acknowledgment (Account 3): At the end of each shift, identify one thing you did well. Not solved or fixed – just handled with competence. Build the habit of noticing your effectiveness, even in small moments.

Centering Breath (All Accounts): When you feel disconnected from purpose, take 2 minutes for the centering breath practice: slow breaths while asking 'Why am I here?' Let the question reconnect you to what matters.

15-Minute-Deep Practice

For when you can go deeper.

Why Essay (Account 1): Write a one-page answer to the question: 'Why do I do this work?' Don't write what sounds good – write what's true for you right now. Revisit and revise this periodically as your why evolves.

Credo Development (Account 1): Write your personal credo: What do you believe about the world? What do you value? Why are you here? Start each statement with 'I believe...' This becomes your anchor when circumstances shake you.

Honor Roll (Account 2): List people outside your profession who exhibit qualities you admire – integrity, kindness, service. Then choose one and reach out: have coffee, ask questions, let their example replenish your belief in people.

Energy Audit (Account 3): List the things, people, and situations that drain your spiritual energy – the 'vampires' that leave you depleted. For each one, identify which account it drains and one thing you could do to protect yourself.

30-Minute Full Engagement

For dedicated spiritual development.

Legacy Letter (Account 1): Write a letter to someone who will outlive you – a child, grandchild, or future family member – explaining why you chose this profession and what you hope your service contributed to the world. This clarifies your why more powerfully than any abstract exercise.

Immersion Experience (Account 2): Spend time in a place where people serve selflessly: a soup kitchen, a hospice, a community organization. Not to help (though you can), but to observe. Let their service remind you what humanity is capable of at its best.

Transition Ritual Design (All Accounts): Develop a complete pre-shift and post-shift transition ritual. Write out each step: what you do, what you say to yourself, how you mark the boundary between roles. Practice for two weeks and note the impact.

Chaplain Conversation (All Accounts): Schedule time with your department chaplain or a counselor who understands first responder spirituality. Share what you're experiencing without editing. Let someone trained in this dimension of wellness help you see what you might be missing.

Sample Credo: Law Enforcement

> I believe in the value of human life.
>
> I believe I was made to defend it.
>
> I believe my life is made more valuable by serving others.
>
> I believe I was given strength, resilience, and compassion to protect those with different gifts.
>
> I believe there is honor in sacrifice.
>
> I believe the weight of this burden is known and seen.
>
> I believe my service matters, even when I can't see the results.

When Spiritual Bankruptcy Approaches

> If you find yourself in deep spiritual overdraft – or worse, bankruptcy – please hear this:
>
> You are not broken. You are depleted.
>
> You didn't do something wrong. You gave more than you received.
>
> This state is not permanent. Spiritual capital can be rebuilt.

But if you're experiencing hopelessness, questioning whether your life matters, or thinking about ending your service (or your life), please reach out:

Safe Call Now: 1-206-459-3020 (24/7, first responder specific)

988 Suicide & Crisis Lifeline

Your department chaplain or peer support

The path back exists. You don't have to walk it alone

Chapter Seven Reflection

Consider these questions honestly. Your answers are for you alone.

- Which spiritual account feels most depleted right now? (Connection to something greater / Belief in people / Confidence in yourself)
- What was your original 'why' for entering this profession? Is it still your why today?
- What experiences have made the largest withdrawals from your spiritual accounts?
- Where would you place yourself: Abundance, Overdraft, or approaching Bankruptcy?
- What is one thing you could do this week to make a deposit in your most depleted account?
- What transition ritual could help you protect your spiritual health?

Chapter Eight

Stewarding Financial & Economic Wealth

Adversity: Dangerous Behaviors & Self-Sabotage

At some point in this profession, almost everyone develops a coping mechanism that does more harm than good. The stress has to go somewhere. The pain must be managed somehow. And the options that provide immediate relief are rarely the ones that serve your long-term wellbeing.

For generations, the default coping mechanism in first responder culture has been alcohol. It was built into the culture – the after-shift drink, the bar where everyone gathered, the unspoken understanding that this was how you processed what you'd seen. But dangerous behaviors extend far beyond alcohol, and they're evolving with each generation that enters the profession.

This chapter addresses two interconnected realities: the behaviors that sabotage your health and career, and the financial foundation that either protects you from their consequences or collapses under their weight. Because here's the truth – dangerous behaviors and financial instability feed each other. Financial stress drives destructive coping. Destructive coping destroys financial stability. Breaking one cycle often requires addressing both.

The Changing Face of Dangerous Behaviors

The specific dangers vary by generation, but the underlying pattern remains constant: stress seeks an outlet, and without healthy options, unhealthy ones fill the void.

The Traditional Pattern: Alcohol

Alcohol remains the most accepted coping mechanism in first responder culture. It's legal, socially normalized, and devastatingly effective at numbing pain in the short term. The sad truth is that most first responder suicides involve alcohol – either as a chronic factor eroding judgment over time or as the accelerant in a moment of crisis.

The warning signs are familiar: needing a drink to unwind, increasing tolerance, drinking alone, hiding consumption from family, showing up to work affected. What starts as social drinking after difficult shifts becomes dependency that's invisible until it isn't.

The Emerging Pattern: Cannabis

As marijuana legalization spreads, cannabis use is increasingly common among younger first responders – often as a perceived "safer" alternative to alcohol. The reasoning seems logical: no hangovers, no liver damage, no bar fights.

But cannabis carries its own risks, particularly for those in high-stakes professions. Regular use affects cognitive function, reaction time, and motivation. It can mask underlying anxiety and depression rather than addressing them. And in most jurisdictions, it remains incompatible with employment in public safety – creating a career-ending risk that's easy to minimize until it's too late.

If you're using cannabis to cope with job stress, the question isn't whether it's "better" than alcohol. The question is what's driving the need to alter your state, and whether you're addressing that root cause or just managing symptoms.

The Hidden Pattern: Food

Food addiction is the dangerous behavior no one talks about – partly because eating is necessary, partly because the consequences are slower to manifest, and partly because first responder culture often celebrates unhealthy eating as part of the job.

The drive-through at 3 AM. The gas station snacks between calls. Stress eating after a difficult shift. The comfort food that's the only pleasure in an otherwise depleting day. Over time, these patterns compound into weight gain, metabolic dysfunction, and chronic health conditions that shorten careers and lives.

For younger generations especially, food has become a primary coping mechanism – perhaps because it's accessible, legal, and carries less immediate stigma than substances. But the long-term costs are just as real: diabetes, cardiovascular disease, joint problems, sleep apnea, and the career limitations that come with failing physical fitness standards.

Generational Shifts in Risk Behavior

Research reveals fascinating differences in how generations cope with stress:

Gen X and older Millennials: Higher rates of alcohol use, often following cultural patterns established in their departments

Younger Millennials: Mixed patterns – some following traditional alcohol use, others gravitating toward cannabis or prescription medications

Gen Z: Lower rates of alcohol consumption and sexual risk-taking than previous generations at the same age – but higher rates of emotional eating, social media dependency, and anxiety-driven behaviors.

A note on younger mission-critical staff: Some "anxiety-driven" behaviors may reflect understimulation. New employees often spend months or years in training, probation, and limited-responsibility roles before being trusted with the work they're wired for. The restlessness and coping behaviors that emerge during this phase may not indicate anxiety – they may indicate a nervous system waiting to be fully engaged.

The takeaway: Dangerous behaviors adapt to the times, but the underlying need they're meeting – escape from pain, relief from stress, something to fill the void – remains constant across generations.

Other Patterns to Watch

Gambling: The rush of risk provides a familiar adrenaline hit for those whose nervous systems are calibrated for high-stakes environments. Online gambling has made this more accessible and easier to hide than ever.

Danger-seeking: Activities that flood the system with adrenaline – reckless driving, extreme sports without proper precautions, picking fights, risky sexual encounters. These often look like courage or vitality, but they're frequently attempts to recreate the chemical state that feels "normal" after years of high-stress work.

Gaming and screen addiction: Hours disappearing into video games, social media, or streaming content. The dopamine hits are reliable and the escape is complete – but relationships, sleep, and real-world engagement erode.

Workaholism: There are two patterns here that look identical but have different roots. The first is overtime as avoidance – staying at work because home is harder, because relationships have atrophied, because the job is the only place you feel valuable. This pattern is genuinely dangerous.

The second pattern is different: work may be the only place you're still challenged, still growing, still using what you're capable of. If everything outside work feels flat and meaningless, the issue may not be that you're avoiding life – it may be that your life outside work doesn't offer anything that matches your wiring. The intervention isn't necessarily working less; it may be building a life outside work that engages you.

The Common Thread

Whatever form dangerous behavior takes, the mechanism is the same: your brain is seeking relief, and it's found something that provides immediate reward without immediate consequence. The problem is that consequences accumulate. By the time they become visible – the DUI, the failed physical, the divorce papers, the empty bank account – the pattern is deeply entrenched.

Early warning signs across all dangerous behaviors include needing more of the behavior to achieve the same relief, difficulty controlling or stopping, continuing despite negative consequences, and withdrawal symptoms (physical or emotional) when the behavior isn't available.

When Dangerous Behaviors Signal Something Different

The pattern above – stress seeking relief through immediate reward – explains most dangerous behaviors. But for the four percent, there's another pattern worth examining: behaviors that look like escape but are attempts to meet legitimate needs.

Research on sensation-seeking shows that people wired for high-stakes work have neurobiological differences in how they process stimulation. They require novelty, challenge, and intensity to feel engaged. When their work stops providing these – when it becomes routine, bureaucratic, or constrained – their nervous system doesn't stop needing stimulation. It just finds it elsewhere.

The firefighter who takes up increasingly extreme hobbies. The officer who picks fights off duty. The paramedic who can't stop gaming. These may not be escaping stress – they may be seeking the engagement their work no longer provides.

This reframe matters because the interventions differ. Classic stress-driven coping benefits from rest, boundaries, and healthier relief mechanisms. Understimulation-driven behavior benefits from finding *legitimate* sources of challenge – meaningful work, demanding hobbies, goals that require everything you have. The question isn't just "what are you running from?" but also "what are you running *toward* that you're not finding in healthy places?"

Getting Help

Culturally competent help exists:

Safe Call Now: 1-206-459-3020 (24/7, first responder specific)

First Responders Children's Foundation: Support for families

Your department's EAP or peer support program

The most important step is finding providers who understand first responder culture. Generic addiction treatment often fails because it doesn't account for the unique stressors, culture, and identity issues involved in this work.

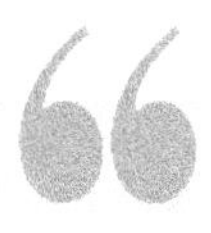

Money is a terrible master, but an excellent servant.

– **P.T. Barnum**

The Financial Foundation

Now we turn to the other half of this chapter – not because finances are separate from dangerous behaviors, but because they're deeply connected. Financial stress is one of the most common triggers for destructive coping. And financial stability is one of the most powerful protections against the desperation that drives poor choices.

Here's something that might surprise you: a career in public safety is one of the most reliable paths to financial security available to people without advanced degrees. Stable income, pension benefits, health insurance, and job security that most private-sector workers can only dream of. The catch is that you have to leverage these advantages instead of squandering them.

The Public Safety Wealth Advantage

Recent workforce research reveals that employees across industries are increasingly prioritizing two things: longevity (job security and stable career paths) and financial security (predictable income and retirement benefits).

Public safety careers offer both – often better than any alternative available to people at similar education levels:

- Defined benefit pensions (increasingly rare in private sector)
- Health insurance that continues into retirement

- Disability protections specific to the profession
- Stable employment even during economic downturns
- Opportunities for overtime and secondary employment

Union representation protecting wages and benefits

The irony: many first responders don't recognize the wealth-building advantages they have until they've squandered them.

Building Wealth on a Public Safety Salary

Let's be direct: you can become a millionaire on a first responder salary. Not through luck or inheritance, but through consistent, disciplined wealth-building over the course of your career. The math works in your favor if you understand it.

The Millionaire Math

If you start at age 25 and invest $500 per month in a diversified portfolio averaging 7% annual returns, you'll have over $1.2 million by age 60. Increase that to $750 per month and you're looking at $1.8 million. These aren't fantasy numbers – they're what happens when you combine time, consistency, and compound growth.

The pension you're earning adds to this. A 30-year career with a 2.5% per year pension formula gives you 75% of your final salary – for life. That's the equivalent of having millions more in retirement accounts.

Add Social Security benefits, and most first responders who manage their money well retire with more financial security than private-sector workers earning twice their salary.

Why Most Don't Get There

If the math works, why do so many first responders struggle financially? The obstacles are predictable:

- Lifestyle inflation – Raises and overtime go to bigger trucks and nicer houses instead of investments
- Divorce – The number one wealth destroyer in this profession
- Dangerous behaviors – Addiction, gambling, and compulsive spending drain accounts
- Lack of financial education – No one teaches this in the academy
- Short-term thinking – Retirement feels too far away to prioritize
- Peer pressure – Keeping up with colleagues who are also making poor choices

Every one of these obstacles is addressable. None of them are inevitable. But addressing them requires intentionality that doesn't come naturally when you're exhausted from shift work and traumatized by what you've witnessed.

> **FIELD PERSPECTIVE**
>
> *"I made sergeant salary for fifteen years and retired with almost nothing. Boat payments, truck payments, a divorce, and too many nights at the bar. Meanwhile, a buddy of mine who made less than me the whole time retired with over a million in investments plus his pension. Same job, completely different outcomes. The difference was choices."*
>
> **– Retired Lieutenant, 28 years of service**

The Wealth-Building Mindset

Before we get to tactics, we need to address mindset – because all the budgeting advice in the world won't help if you're operating from beliefs that sabotage wealth-building.

From Scarcity to Abundance

Many first responders operate from a scarcity mindset: there's never enough, money is stressful, wealth is for other people. This mindset becomes self-fulfilling. If you believe you can't build wealth, you won't take the actions that build wealth.

The shift to abundance isn't about ignoring financial realities – it's about recognizing the genuine advantages you have and acting on them. You have stable income. You have benefits most workers don't. You have time (a 20–30-year career) that makes compound growth possible. You have more than enough to build substantial wealth if you choose to.

From Spending to Investing

The wealthiest people – regardless of income level – think differently about money. When they receive income, their first question isn't "What can I buy?" but "What can I invest?" They pay themselves first, putting money into wealth-building vehicles before spending on anything discretionary.

This requires a fundamental shift: seeing saving not as deprivation but as paying your future self. Every dollar you invest today is a dollar that will work for you for decades. Every dollar you spend on something depreciating is gone forever.

From Consumption to Creation

The traditional advice says save 15% of your income. That's a good start. But if you want to accelerate wealth-building, consider creating additional income streams rather than just cutting expenses.

First responders have unique advantages here: skills that translate to security consulting, training, and private sector roles. Schedules that allow for side businesses. Credibility that opens doors. The question isn't whether opportunities exist – it's whether you're positioning yourself to capture them.

For Younger First Responders

You have the most powerful wealth-building asset of all: time. Here's what that means in practical terms:

Starting at 22 vs 32: Investing $400/month starting at 22 gives you roughly DOUBLE what starting at 32 gives you by age 60 – even though you only invested 40% more money. That's compound growth.

The pension advantage: Every year of service counts. A full 30-year career at one agency maximizes your pension benefit. Job-hopping has costs that aren't immediately visible.

Non-traditional wealth building: Consider real estate (house hacking, rental properties), index fund investing (simple and effective), Roth accounts (tax-free growth), side businesses that leverage your skills.

The millionaire goal is realistic: If reaching millionaire status by retirement is your goal, you're in the right profession to achieve it. But you have to start now, not someday.

Practical Wealth Stewardship

Mindset matters, but so does execution. Here are the practical foundations of wealth-building in public safety careers.

Step 1: Know Your Numbers

You can't manage what you don't measure. Before any other financial move, you need clarity on three numbers: what comes in, what goes out, and what's left.

Most people dramatically underestimate their spending. The daily coffee, the subscription services, the impulse Amazon purchases – they add up to hundreds or thousands per month that could be building wealth instead.

Use whatever system works for you – apps like YNAB or Mint, a spreadsheet, or old-school pen and paper. The method matters less than the habit of tracking.

Step 2: Eliminate Wealth Destroyers

Some financial choices are obvious wealth destroyers:

- High-interest debt (credit cards, payday loans) – Pay these off aggressively before other financial priorities
- Depreciating assets financed at high interest – That $60,000 truck at 8% interest is costing you far more than the sticker price
- Lifestyle creep – Every raise going to more stuff instead of more security
- Financial enabling – Bailing out family members repeatedly with no plan for change

The rule of thumb: if it loses value over time and you're paying interest on it, it's actively working against your wealth-building.

Step 3: Automate Wealth-Building

Willpower is unreliable. Systems are reliable. Set up automatic transfers so that money moves to savings and investments before you ever see it in your checking account.

- Emergency fund first: 3-6 months of expenses in accessible savings
- Retirement accounts: Max out any employer match (it's free money), then increase contributions annually
- Additional investments: Taxable brokerage accounts, real estate, other vehicles

When saving is automatic, you adjust your lifestyle to what's left rather than saving what's left after lifestyle. The psychological difference is enormous.

Step 4: Protect What You Build

Wealth-building can be undone quickly. Protect your progress:

- Insurance: Life insurance if others depend on your income, disability insurance beyond what your employer provides, umbrella liability coverage
- Estate planning: Will, beneficiary designations, powers of attorney – even if you're young and single
- Marriage protection: Have honest financial conversations before marriage; consider the implications of divorce on pensions and assets
- Boundary-setting: Decide now what you're willing to do financially for family members, and communicate it.

FIELD PERSPECTIVE

"I'm 27 and already maxing my Roth IRA and getting the full pension match. My older coworkers think I'm crazy for not enjoying my money while I'm young. But I did the math – if I keep this up, I'll have options at 50 that they won't have at 60. That's not deprivation, that's freedom."

– Deputy Sheriff, 4 years of service

Beyond Personal Finance: Economic Capital

Financial capital is what you own. Economic capital is what you have access to – the broader network of resources, relationships, and opportunities that extend beyond your personal accounts.

First responders have unique access to economic capital that most people don't. You interact with every sector of your community: nonprofits, businesses, government agencies, healthcare systems. These connections are valuable – not for exploitation, but for mutual benefit and service.

Building Economic Capital

- Know your community resources: What nonprofits serve your area? What programs exist for housing, food security, mental health, addiction treatment? This knowledge helps the people you serve and builds your network.
- Develop relationships across sectors: The business owner you meet on a call, the nonprofit director who handles your referrals, the hospital administrator you coordinate with – these relationships have value beyond the immediate interaction.
- Consider board service: Many nonprofits need board members with practical community knowledge. Your

perspective is valuable, and board service builds skills and connections.

- Think about Act 2: Your post-retirement career will likely leverage the relationships and knowledge built during your first responder years. Cultivate them intentionally.

Stewardship and Generosity

True wealth isn't just accumulation – it's the capacity to be generous. When your financial foundation is solid, you can give without anxiety: time to causes you believe in, money to organizations that matter, help to people who need it.

This isn't about giving until it hurts. It's about building a position where giving becomes possible, sustainable, and joyful. The first responder who's drowning in debt and stress has nothing left to give. The one who's built financial security can extend that security to others.

The Second Act

Research shows most people experience at least two major careers. For first responders, the pattern is often:

Act 1: The career of necessity and service (your first responder years)

Act 2: The career of passion and choice (what comes after)

Very few first responders fully retire at retirement. They transition to consulting, training, nonprofit work, small businesses, or entirely new fields. The financial decisions you make in Act 1 determine your options in Act 2.

Plan now for what might be a decade or more of post-retirement productivity – and the resources you'll need to pursue it on your own terms.

Activities for Building Financial Capital

When you engage in behaviors you know aren't good for you, are you trying to escape something painful, or are you trying to *feel* something – engagement, challenge, aliveness – that you're not finding elsewhere? Your answer points toward different solutions.

5-Minute Quick Wins

Small actions that build momentum.

The Net Worth Check: Open your phone right now. Add up what you own (accounts, property, investments). Subtract what you owe (loans, credit cards, mortgage). That number is your current net worth. Write it down. Knowing the number is the first step to changing it.

The Subscription Audit: Look at your bank statement for the last month. Circle every recurring charge – streaming services, apps, memberships, subscriptions. How many are you using? Cancel at least one today.

The 24-Hour Rule: Before any non-essential purchase over $50, wait 24 hours. Most impulse buying fades when you create space between desire and purchase. Start this practice today.

The Benefits Check: Do you know what short-term and long-term disability benefits your employer provides? What happens to your income if you're injured? If you don't know, schedule a meeting with HR this week.

15-Minute-Deep Practice

For focused financial development.

The Money Conversation: If you have a partner, schedule 15 minutes to discuss finances – not to solve everything, just to check in. What are you each worried about? What would you each like to prioritize? Regular money conversations prevent financial secrets and conflicts.

The Millionaire Projection: Use an online compound interest calculator. Input your current age, target retirement age, and different monthly investment amounts. See what's possible with consistent investing over your career. Let the math motivate you.

The Wealth Destroyer Inventory: List the financial decisions that are actively working against your wealth-building: high-interest debt, depreciating assets, recurring expenses that don't add value. For each one, write one action you could take to address it.

The Act 2 Vision: Imagine yourself at retirement. What do you want to be doing? What resources would you need? Write a brief description of your ideal Act 2 – then work backward to identify what you'd need to build financially to make it possible.

30-Minute Full Engagement

For comprehensive financial planning.

The Complete Budget Build: Using whatever system works for you, create a complete picture of your monthly income and expenses. Categorize everything. Identify where money is going that doesn't align with your priorities. Make three specific changes.

The Benefits Deep Dive: Schedule a meeting with your HR department. Learn everything about your disability coverage, pension formula, retirement options, and what happens if your career ends unexpectedly. Document what you learn.

The Emergency Plan: If your career ended tomorrow due to injury, what would happen financially? Write out a specific plan: what benefits would kick in, how long they'd last, what you'd need to bridge any gaps. Identify any vulnerabilities and take one action to address them.

The Family Finance Conversation: Discuss with your partner and/or family: What foreseeable family needs might require financial resources (aging parents, children's education, potential crises)? What boundaries will you set? What can you prepare for now? Document your decisions.

The Dangerous Behavior Check-In

As you work on financial health, be honest about whether dangerous behaviors are undermining your progress:

- How much are you spending on alcohol, cannabis, or other substances?
- Are gambling, gaming, or shopping affecting your finances?
- Are you using money to cope with stress in ways that create more stress?

Financial health and behavioral health are connected. Addressing one often requires addressing both.

Chapter Eight Reflection

Consider these questions honestly. Your answers are for you alone.

- What coping behaviors are you using that might be working against your long-term wellbeing?
- What's your current net worth? (Assets minus liabilities)
- Are you on track to reach your financial goals by retirement? If not, what's the gap?
- What's one financial decision you've made that's working against wealth-building?
- What would your Act 2 look like if you had complete financial freedom?
- What one action will you take this week to improve your financial position?

Chapter Nine

Choosing Your Tribe: Building Social Capital

Adversity: Isolation & Loneliness

Here's something the wellness industry rarely tells first responders: the single most important factor in how long you live – and how well you live – isn't your diet, your exercise routine, or even your stress level. It's the quality of your relationships.

This might sound like a soft claim, but the research behind it is some of the most robust in all medical science. And for first responders, whose work can systematically erode relationships while creating an illusion of connection through shared trauma, understanding this research isn't just interesting – it's survival information.

Friendship multiplies the good in life and divides the evil.

– Baltasar Gracián

Longevity Research: Why Relationships Matter More Than You Think

In 1938, Harvard began tracking the health and wellbeing of 724 men – some from Harvard, some from Boston's poorest neighborhoods. The Harvard Study of Adult Development has now followed these men, their spouses, and their children for over 85 years, making it the longest study of adult life ever conducted.

The findings are unambiguous: good relationships keep us healthier and happier. Period.

The people who were most satisfied with their relationships at age 50 were the healthiest at age 80. Close relationships – more than money, fame, social class, genes, or IQ – were the best predictor of who would live long and well. Social connections literally protected their brains; those in quality relationships maintained sharper memory longer.

The opposite was equally clear: loneliness kills. People who were more isolated than they wanted to be were less happy, their health declined earlier in midlife, their brain function declined sooner, and they lived shorter lives.

The Science of Connection

The longevity research extends far beyond Harvard:

- A meta-analysis of 148 studies (308,849 participants) found that people with strong social relationships had a 50% greater likelihood of survival than those with weak or insufficient social relationships.
- The health impact of loneliness is equivalent to smoking 15 cigarettes a day – greater than obesity, physical inactivity, or air pollution.

- Social isolation increases the risk of premature death by 26%, and loneliness by 29%.
- Quality matters more than quantity. Having three close relationships beats having twenty superficial ones.

This isn't correlation. Researchers have identified biological pathways: social connection affects immune function, inflammation levels, cardiovascular health, and even gene expression.

Why This Matters for the Mission-Critical Professional

In this field, you face a paradox: your work creates intense bonds with colleagues who understand what you've experienced – yet it simultaneously erodes the civilian relationships that research shows are essential for long-term health.

The mechanisms are predictable:

- Shift work disrupts family time and social rhythms
- Emotional exhaustion leaves nothing for relationships at home
- Hypervigilance creates distance even when physically present
- Trauma exposure makes 'normal' conversations feel trivial
- The code of silence prevents authentic connection with anyone outside the profession

The result is often a shrinking social world – deep bonds with a few colleagues, deteriorating relationships with everyone else. And while those colleague bonds are valuable, they can't replace the diversity of relationships that promote genuine health and longevity.

The Hidden Relationship Drain: Being Unseen

There's another mechanism eroding first responder relationships that rarely gets named: the experience of being in connection but not being *seen*.

You can have an anchor relationship with someone who loves you deeply but doesn't understand how to show it in a way you can receive. Research on appreciation languages shows that recognition delivered in the wrong "language" – public praise when you need private acknowledgment, words when you need acts of service – falls flat no matter how sincere. Over time, you stop feeling valued even though the other person is trying.

You can have close friends who hurt you and genuinely want to repair the relationship but don't know how to apologize in a way that lands. Research on apology languages shows that people have different requirements for trust repair – some need to hear responsibility taken, others need restitution, others need the behavior to change. When ruptures go unrepaired because the apology doesn't match your needs, relationships erode even when both parties want them to work.

You can be surrounded by people who care about you but fundamentally don't understand your wiring – why you need challenge, why routine feels like suffocation, why you can't just "relax" the way they do.

If your relationships feel hollow despite genuine effort from both sides, the issue may not be quantity or even authenticity. It may be fit – whether the people in your life have the tools to see and honor who you are.

FROM THE COMM CENTER

"People think dispatchers have it easier socially because we're not on the street. But we work alone in a dark room listening to the worst moments of people's lives, then go home to families who can't understand why we're distracted. My husband stopped asking about my day years ago. I'm surrounded by voices all shift, then completely alone in my own house."

– 911 Dispatcher, 9 years of service

The Circles of Connection

Understanding your social world requires mapping it honestly. Not everyone in your life serves the same function, and not every relationship requires the same investment.

Anchors

These are your closest relationships – the people who hold you steady regardless of circumstances. Typically limited to a handful of people: perhaps a spouse, a parent, a sibling, or a lifelong friend. Anchors provide what researchers call a 'secure base' – the knowledge that someone has your back unconditionally.

The Harvard study was clear: it's not the number of anchors that matters, but the security of the attachment. One solid anchor relationship can be more protective than a dozen casual friendships.

Warning signs that anchor relationships are eroding: you've stopped sharing what's really going on; you default to surface conversations; you spend time in the same space but aren't truly connecting; you feel more alone in their presence than when alone.

Close Friends

Beyond anchors are close friends – people you've chosen, who share your values and experiences, with whom you can be authentic. Research suggests most people maintain 3-5 close friendships at any given time, though these may shift across life stages.

For first responders, the strongest friendships often form through shared high-stakes experiences. Military veterans describe bonds forged in combat that nothing can break. First responders experience similar bonding through shared calls, shared trauma, shared understanding.

These bonds are real and valuable. But they can also create an insular world where your entire social circle consists of people who share your trauma, your cynicism, and your coping mechanisms. Diversity in friendship – people from different worlds, different perspectives, different experiences – is protective in ways that an echo chamber cannot be.

FIELD PERSPECTIVE

"After my divorce, I realized my only friends were cops. Every one of them. When I started going to church again, I felt like an alien. But those people – the ones who didn't understand my job at all – ended up saving my life. They saw me as a person, not just a badge."

– Patrol Officer, 19 years of service

Acquaintances and Weak Ties

Sociology research has revealed something counterintuitive: your acquaintances – the 'weak ties' in your network – often provide more value than your close relationships for certain purposes. Job opportunities, new information, fresh perspectives, and exposure to different ways of thinking typically come through weak ties rather than close friends.

First responders often let these weak ties atrophy. The neighbor you used to chat with, the gym buddy from before you started shift work, the college friend you've lost touch with – these connections feel expendable when you're exhausted. But they represent pathways to opportunity and perspective that your close circle can't provide.

Energy Vampires

Not everyone deserves a place in your tribe. Energy vampires are people who drain you without reciprocating – those who create drama, who always need something from you, who leave you feeling worse after every interaction.

In first responder culture, energy vampires often hide behind cynicism and dark humor. They're the ones who make everything negative, who tear down colleagues rather than building them up, who spread gossip and resentment. Their presence in your social circle isn't neutral – it actively harms your wellbeing and everyone else's.

Setting boundaries with energy vampires isn't cruel; it's necessary. Your social energy is limited, and every hour spent with someone who drains you is an hour not spent with someone who fills you.

A note of nuance: not everyone who drains you is an energy vampire in the toxic sense. Sometimes the drain comes from relationships that require you to be someone you're not – suppressing your intensity, performing emotions you don't feel, pretending to care about things that bore you. These aren't bad people; they're mismatched connections. The relationship might be salvageable if you can be more authentically yourself, or it might be one where genuine connection simply isn't possible given who you each are. Distinguishing between toxic people and mismatched connections helps you respond appropriately – boundaries with vampires, renegotiation or acceptance with mismatches.

Connection in the Digital Age

Here's where the conversation gets interesting – and where many experts get it wrong.

The common narrative says that digital connection is inferior to 'real' connection, that social media is destroying relationships, that young people don't know how to connect anymore. This narrative is incomplete at best and harmful at worst.

The Reality of Online Relationships

Research increasingly supports what many young people already know: online relationships can be genuine, meaningful, and protective.

A 2022 study in the Journal of Computer-Mediated Communication found that online friendships can provide the same emotional support and sense of belonging as in-person relationships. For people with niche interests, social anxiety, or geographic limitations, online communities may be the primary source of meaningful connection.

Consider gaming communities. To outsiders, they might look like people staring at screens. But inside those communities are genuine friendships, shared experiences, mutual support, and regular communication. The fact that the connection happens through a game rather than a coffee shop doesn't make it less real.

The Value of Virtual Community

For younger first responders especially, online relationships deserve recognition:

Discord servers, gaming communities, and online groups can provide:

- Consistent social contact despite shift work schedules
- Connections with people who share specific interests
- A space to decompress that doesn't require physical energy
- Anonymity to discuss struggles without professional stigma
- Friendships that transcend geography

The research is clear: what matters is the quality of connection, not the medium. A supportive online friend you talk to daily may provide more health benefit than a local acquaintance you see occasionally.

The key is intentionality. Passive scrolling isn't connection. Active engagement in communities that matter to you is.

FROM THE COMM CENTER

"My best friends are people I've never met in person. We're all dispatchers in different states, connected through a Discord server. We understand each other's bad shifts. We celebrate each other's wins. We've talked people through crises. I don't care if my older coworkers think it's weird – these people have kept me in this profession."

– 911 Telecommunicator, 4 years of service

The Social Media Distinction

There's an important difference between active online connection and passive social media consumption.

Active connection – messaging friends, participating in communities, engaging in meaningful exchanges – has positive health effects similar to in-person relationships.

Passive consumption – scrolling feeds, comparing your life to curated highlight reels, absorbing negativity without engaging – tends to increase loneliness and depression rather than alleviating it.

For first responders, social media carries additional risks: exposure to criticism of your profession, secondhand trauma from viral content, and the temptation to post things that damage your career. Being intentional about how you engage online isn't about being old-fashioned – it's about protecting your wellbeing.

Building Connection When It's Hard

If you're reading this and recognizing that your social world has shrunk, you're not alone. Many first responders reach this point. The question is what to do about it.

The Challenge for Young Adults

Younger first responders face a specific challenge: building in-person relationships has become genuinely harder than they were for previous generations.

The 'third places' – spaces that aren't work or home where organic social connection happened – have largely disappeared. Fewer community organizations, less religious participation, less neighborhood connection, more mobility, and more screen-based leisure have combined to make spontaneous friendship formation rare.

Add shift work to this equation, and the difficulty compounds. You're free when others are working. You're sleeping when others are socializing. Your schedule changes constantly. The traditional pathways to friendship simply don't work.

This isn't a character flaw or a generational weakness. It's a structural reality that requires intentional solutions.

Strategies That Work

Protect anchor relationships fiercely: Whatever your schedule, carve out time for your closest relationships. They're not a luxury you get to when you have time – they're a health requirement as important as sleep.

Diversify your social portfolio: If all your friends are first responders, deliberately cultivate relationships outside the profession. Join something – a gym, a club, a faith community, a class – that puts you in regular contact with people whose worldview differs from yours.

Invest in online community: If your schedule makes in-person connection difficult, build genuine relationships online. Find communities aligned with your interests and engage actively, not passively.

Be the initiator: Waiting for others to reach out is a recipe for isolation. Make the first move. Suggest the gathering. Send the text. Initiate the conversation. The person on the other end is probably waiting for someone to reach out too.

Guard against drift: Relationships don't end dramatically – they fade through neglect. Notice when connections are weakening and take action before they're gone.

FIELD PERSPECTIVE

"I used to think my shift schedule made friendship impossible. Then I found a mountain biking group that rides at 6 AM. Different schedules, but we all carved out that one time. Now I've got friends who have nothing to do with my job, who know nothing about what I see at work. They talk about their kids and their projects and normal stuff. It's like oxygen."

– Firefighter/EMT, 8 years of service

The Social Contract

Every relationship involves an implicit contract – mutual expectations about how you'll treat each other. Most social friction comes from violated expectations that were never made explicit.

In anchor relationships, making the contract explicit is essential. What do you expect from each other? What are your boundaries? How will you communicate about difficult things? What support do you need, and what support can you provide?

For first responders, the social contract often needs to address:

- How you'll share (or not share) details of difficult calls
- How to signal when you need space versus when you need connection
- How to handle schedule disruptions to plans
- What hypervigilance looks like in you and how your partner can respond
- When to push and when to give space

These conversations aren't automatic. They require vulnerability, which is hard for people trained to project strength. But the alternative – assumed expectations leading to repeated disappointment – is far more damaging in the long run.

Beyond these logistics, consider sharing how you best receive support. Do you feel appreciated through words, acts of service, quality time, or something else? When trust is damaged, what do you need to feel it's been repaired – an apology, changed behavior, making things right, or giving it time? These aren't personality quirks; they're wiring differences that, when understood, prevent the frustrating experience of someone trying hard to support you in ways that don't land.

FROM THE COMM CENTER

"The thing nobody tells you is that you can't turn it off. I go home and my husband says something like 'I had a rough day' because traffic was bad, and inside I'm thinking about the father I listened to give CPR to his toddler. I had to learn to tell him: 'I need you to ask me how my day was, but I also need you to be okay if I can't answer.' That conversation changed our marriage."

– Communications Supervisor, 14 years of service

The Loneliness Paradox

Many first responders feel lonely despite being surrounded by people – colleagues on shift, citizens on calls, family at home.

This is because loneliness isn't about physical presence. It's about the gap between the connection you have and the connection you need.

You can feel profoundly alone in a crowd and deeply connected to someone a thousand miles away. The measure isn't proximity – it's authenticity.

If you're feeling lonely, the answer isn't necessarily more social contact. It might be deeper social contact – conversations where you're seen, relationships where you can drop the armor

Activities for Building Social Capital

In your closest relationships, do you feel genuinely *seen* – understood for who you are, not who others expect you to be? If not, is the issue that you haven't revealed yourself, or that they don't have the capacity to see you?

When someone tries to show you appreciation or repair a hurt, does it usually land? If not, have you ever told them what you need?

5-Minute Quick Wins

Small actions that maintain connection.

The Reach-Out: Right now, send a text to someone you haven't connected with in a while. Not asking for anything – just letting them know you're thinking of them. Do this once per day for a week and notice what happens.

The Gratitude Message: Think of someone who has positively impacted your life. Send them a message telling them specifically what they did and how it affected you. This strengthens the relationship for both of you.

The Presence Check: When you're with someone you care about, put your phone completely away. Give them five minutes of undivided attention. Notice how different the interaction feels.

The Social Inventory: Quickly list your anchors, close friends, and acquaintances. When did you last have meaningful contact with each? Are any relationships in danger of drifting away?

15-Minute-Deep Practice

For intentional relationship development.

The Social Map: Draw three concentric circles. In the center, write your anchors. In the middle ring, close friends. In the outer ring, acquaintances. Looking at this map: Is there enough diversity? Are all circles adequately filled? What does this reveal about your social health?

The Energy Audit: List the people you spend the most time with. For each one, rate whether time with them typically leaves you energized (+), drained (−), or neutral (0). What does this tell you about where to invest your limited social energy?

The Contract Conversation: With one anchor relationship, have an explicit conversation about expectations. What do you each need from the relationship? What boundaries matter? How do you want to handle conflict? This conversation may feel awkward but creates clarity that prevents future friction.

The New Connection Plan: Identify one way you could meet new people whose schedules and interests align with yours. Research specific options: What groups exist? When do they meet? What would it take to show up?

30-Minute Full Engagement

For comprehensive social development.

The Relationship History: Write the story of one important relationship: how it started, how it's evolved, what it provides for you and what you provide for them. What has made it strong? What has threatened it? What would make it even better?

The Loneliness Exploration: If you've been feeling lonely, spend time writing about it. When does the loneliness hit? What kind of connection are you missing? What's standing in the way? What's one thing you could do to address it?

The Diversification Project: If your social world has become insular, plan a diversification project. What community could you join that would expose you to different people and perspectives? Commit to trying it for at least a month.

The Digital Audit: Review your online presence. Where are you actively connecting versus passively consuming? What communities provide genuine support? What feeds or platforms leave you feeling worse? Make three specific changes to how you engage online.

Chapter Nine Reflection

Consider these questions honestly. Your answers are for you alone.

- Who are your anchors – the people who would be there for you no matter what?
- When did you last have a truly authentic conversation where you were fully seen?
- Has your social world expanded or contracted since entering this profession?
- Do you have meaningful relationships outside of first responder circles?
- What online communities or relationships provide genuine support for you?
- What one action could you take this week to strengthen your social capital?

Chapter Ten

Building Professional Capital: Influence, Culture & Legacy

Adversity: Organizational Toxicity & Cynicism

Research consistently shows that organizational stressors – toxic leadership, broken systems, lack of support, and cultural dysfunction – cause more lasting psychological harm than exposure to traumatic incidents. This is a stunning finding that many departments refuse to acknowledge.

You can survive terrible calls. You can process trauma, build resilience, and continue to serve. What's harder to survive is working for years in an environment where your leadership doesn't support you, your colleagues tear each other down, and the culture punishes authenticity while rewarding cynicism.

This chapter is about professional capital – the value of your workplace relationships and your ability to influence the culture you work in. Unlike social capital, which is about the relationships you choose, professional capital is partly shaped by circumstances beyond your control. But your influence within that environment is far greater than you might think.

The greatest good you can do for another is not just to share your riches, but to reveal to him his own.

– Benjamin Disraeli

The Two Types of Professional Stress

First responders face two distinct categories of stress, and confusing them leads to misguided solutions.

Occupational Stress

This is the stress that comes with the job itself – the danger, the trauma, the weight of life-and-death decisions. When you chose this profession, you accepted occupational stress. You knew firefighting would mean entering burning buildings. You knew policing would mean confronting violence. You knew dispatching would mean hearing people's worst moments through a headset.

Occupational stress is manageable. It's what training prepares you for. It's what your colleagues understand because they face it too. It's demanding, but it's what you signed up for – and it's part of what gives the work meaning.

Organizational Stress

This is the stress that comes from how your agency is run – the policies that don't make sense, the leaders who don't lead, the colleagues who undermine rather than support, the systems that punish those who speak up.

Organizational stress is different. It's avoidable. It's not inherent to the work – it's a function of how work environments are managed. And unlike occupational stress, it often comes without warning and without tools to address it.

Examples of organizational stressors include:

- Lack of transparency in leadership decision-making
- Favoritism in assignments, promotions, and discipline
- Outdated policies that create obstacles rather than solutions
- Inadequate staffing forcing unsafe workloads
- Stigma around mental health and help-seeking
- Toxic colleagues protected by seniority or connections
- Punishment for pointing out problems

When researchers study first responder wellness, organizational stress emerges as more damaging than traumatic exposure. This means you can work in a high-call-volume environment and thrive if the culture is healthy – or deteriorate in a low-call-volume environment if the culture is toxic.

The Hidden Organizational Stressor: Being Treated Like Everyone Else

There's a category of organizational stress that rarely appears on any list but may be the most damaging for the four percent: being treated generically.

You were selected for this profession because you're wired differently. Higher sensation-seeking. Greater tolerance for risk. A need for meaningful challenge that would overwhelm most people. These aren't just personality traits – they're neurobiological differences that affect how you experience work, recognition, and relationships.

When organizations treat the 4% like the 96%, a predictable cascade follows:

Recognition falls flat because it's delivered in the wrong "appreciation language" – public praise when you need private acknowledgment, verbal recognition when you need increased responsibility.

Trust ruptures go unrepaired because supervisors and colleagues don't know how to apologize in ways you can receive – they say the words without taking responsibility, or take responsibility without changing behavior.

Work assignments don't match your wiring – you're given routine tasks when you need challenge, or micromanaged when you need autonomy.

Over time, you stop feeling seen. Psychological safety erodes. You disengage not because the work is too hard, but because the environment doesn't recognize who you are.

This form of organizational stress is particularly insidious because it's invisible. No policy created it. No leader intended it. It's simply the result of one-size-fits-all management applied to people who don't fit the standard size.

FROM THE COMM CENTER

"The hard calls? I can handle those. What I can't handle is my supervisor taking credit for my work, the schedule being manipulated to punish people who complain, and being written up for taking bathroom breaks during a twelve-hour shift. The job doesn't burn me out – the building does."

– Senior Dispatcher, 11 years of service

Organizational Betrayal

The deepest wounds in first responder careers often come from organizational betrayal – being harmed by the very institution you sacrificed to serve.

Betrayal by strangers is expected. You're trained for it. But betrayal by your department – the leaders you trusted, the colleagues you relied on, the institution you gave yourself to – strikes at something fundamental. It's experienced not just as a professional setback but as a personal violation.

Examples of organizational betrayal include:

- Being disciplined for following policy while others violate it without consequence
- Having your career derailed for seeking mental health support
- Discovering that leadership knew about a danger and didn't warn you
- Being scapegoated for systemic failures
- Watching colleagues harass or harm others while administration looks away
- Having your concerns dismissed, minimized, or punished

Betrayal doesn't always arrive as a single event. Sometimes it's chronic – the slow realization that the organization will never see you as an individual. Year after year of recognition that doesn't land. Repeated experiences of raising concerns and being dismissed. The gradual understanding that no matter how much you give, you'll be treated the same as someone giving nothing.

This chronic form of betrayal is harder to name because there's no specific incident to point to. But the cumulative effect can be just as damaging – a deep erosion of trust that makes genuine engagement feel impossible.

The psychological research on institutional betrayal shows that it compounds trauma. A traumatic event is harder to heal from when it occurs within an institution that should have protected you and didn't. The injury and the betrayal reinforce each other.

RODGER'S REFLECTION

After my diagnosis, my department's response taught me more about organizational culture than any training ever had. Some leaders supported me – genuinely wanted me to get well and return. Others saw me as a liability to be managed. And the whisper campaigns among colleagues showed me who had my back and who saw my struggle as their opportunity. The trauma of Stonypoint and Hearn was overwhelming. But the professional isolation that followed the diagnosis left a different kind of scar – one that took just as long to heal.

The Cynicism Epidemic

One of the most dangerous professional adversities you'll face isn't a policy or a leader – it's the learned cynicism that spreads through first responder culture like a virus.

Skepticism vs. Cynicism

There's an important distinction between healthy skepticism and destructive cynicism:

The skeptic questions people and verifies facts. They maintain appropriate doubt while remaining open to evidence.

The cynic doubts facts and dismisses people. They assume the worst about everyone and everything, and no evidence can change their mind.

Skepticism is a professional skill. When you're investigating a crime or assessing a scene, you should question what you're told. When a policy is proposed, you should ask who benefits and what could go wrong. This is wisdom.

Cynicism is a professional poison. When you can no longer believe that anyone has good intentions, when every policy is assumed to be manipulation, when every colleague is seen as competition or threat – you've moved from skepticism to cynicism. And cynicism doesn't just affect your work; it spreads to everyone around you.

The Cynicism Test

> How do you know if you've crossed from skepticism to cynicism?
>
> Ask yourself: Can I imagine evidence that would change my mind?
>
> The skeptic can always answer yes. They might be doubtful, but they remain open to being convinced.
>
> The cynic's answer is no. Their conclusions are fixed. No evidence will persuade them because they've already decided that all evidence is suspect.
>
> If you find yourself in conversations where nothing anyone says could possibly change your view, you're not being appropriately cautious – you're being cynical. And cynicism, unlike skepticism, destroys both the cynic and everyone who has to work with them.

How Cynicism Spreads

Nobody enters this profession cynical. You were idealistic once – believing you could make a difference, protect the innocent, serve your community. That idealism was part of why you were suited for this work.

Cynicism is learned. It's taught by colleagues who've given up but stayed in the job. It's reinforced by organizational failures that punish the good and reward the political. It's spread through break room conversations where tearing down is easier than building up.

The pattern is predictable: you enter idealistic, encounter disappointments that weren't addressed in training, look to more experienced colleagues for guidance, and absorb their perspective on how the world really works. If those colleagues are healthy skeptics, you learn wisdom. If they're cynics, you learn cynicism.

This is why the cynics in your organization are so dangerous – not just to themselves, but to every person who comes after them. They're training the next generation to see the world as they do.

When Cynicism is a Rational Response

There's another pathway to cynicism that deserves acknowledgment: sometimes it emerges from accurate perception being repeatedly dismissed.

The four percent often see organizational dysfunction clearly. They recognize broken systems, ineffective leadership, and cultural problems before others do. When they raise these concerns and are told they have an "attitude problem"... when their frustration is labeled as "not being a team player"... when accurate perception is pathologized as negativity... cynicism becomes an understandable response.

This doesn't make cynicism healthy or useful. But it does suggest that some cynics aren't people who gave up too easily – they're people who saw clearly, spoke up, were dismissed, and eventually stopped believing anyone would listen.

If you recognize this pattern in yourself, the path forward isn't simply to "be more positive." It's to find environments where accurate perception is valued, or to channel your clear-sightedness into influence rather than withdrawal. The cynic and the change agent often see the same problems – the difference is what they do with what they see.

FIELD PERSPECTIVE

"My first FTO told me on day one: 'Forget everything they taught you in the academy. Everyone lies. Everyone's guilty of something. Trust no one.' I spent the next ten years living that philosophy. It made me a terrible cop and destroyed my marriage. The tragedy is that I passed that same message to rookies I trained. I was creating copies of my own dysfunction."

– Retired Sergeant, 22 years of service

Building Healthy Professional Relationships

Despite the challenges, your professional relationships can be a source of strength rather than stress. The key is intentionality – choosing who you invest in and how you show up.

The People Who Matter

Not everyone in your professional world deserves the same investment. Some relationships are strategic – connections that advance your career or help you do your job. Others are authentic – colleagues who become genuine friends. And some are simply proximity – people you work with without meaningful connection.

Identify the people who genuinely support your growth and wellbeing. These are the colleagues who:

- Celebrate your successes without jealousy
- Offer honest feedback without cruelty
- Have your back when you're not in the room
- Challenge your thinking without dismissing your perspective
- Maintain their integrity under pressure

These people are your professional anchors. Invest in them deliberately. Their presence in your professional life is as protective as anchors in your personal life.

Navigating Toxic Colleagues

You don't get to choose all your colleagues, and some will be actively harmful. Energy vampires who drain everyone around them. Cynics who poison morale. Political players who manipulate for personal advantage. People who simply shouldn't be in this profession but are protected by systems that won't remove them.

You can't change these people. But you can limit their impact:

- Minimize unnecessary interaction while remaining professional
- Don't engage in their negativity or gossip
- Document interactions when appropriate
- Build relationships around them so their influence is diluted

- Refuse to pass on their cynicism to those coming behind you

The goal isn't to reform toxic colleagues – it's to protect yourself and others from their influence while doing your job with integrity.

FROM THE COMM CENTER

"There's one person in our center who's been there forever and hates everyone. For years, I let her set the tone of my shift. I'd come in positive and leave defeated just from absorbing her negativity. Now I'm cordial but boundaried. I don't engage when she starts complaining. I redirect when she gossips. It took practice, but I stopped letting someone else's misery dictate my experience."

– 911 Telecommunicator, 7 years of service

Your Influence on Culture

Here's what most first responders don't realize: you have far more influence on your organization's culture than you think.

Culture isn't set by mission statements or policy manuals. It's set by thousands of daily interactions – how people treat each other, what behaviors are accepted or challenged, what gets talked about in the break room. Every person in an organization contributes to culture through their words and actions.

This means you have a choice. You can absorb and amplify the toxic elements of your culture – becoming another voice for cynicism, another example of self-interest, another person who tears down rather than builds up. Or you can be a counterforce – modeling integrity, supporting colleagues, challenging negativity, and creating pockets of health even in unhealthy environments.

Practical Influence

You don't need rank to influence culture. You can:

- Be the person who refuses to participate in gossip
- Offer genuine support to struggling colleagues instead of judgment
- Acknowledge good work in others – publicly and privately
- Challenge cynical generalizations with specific counterexamples
- Model healthy help-seeking by being open about your own struggles
- Train those who come after you with wisdom rather than bitterness

These actions seem small, but they compound. One person who consistently models integrity creates permission for others to do the same. And over time, those pockets of health can grow.

The Ripple Effect

Research on organizational culture shows that individual behavior spreads through networks.

Positive behavior is contagious. When you treat colleagues with respect, they're more likely to treat others with respect. When you model healthy boundaries, others learn they're possible.

Negative behavior is contagious too. When you participate in cynicism, you're giving permission to others to be cynical. When you tear down colleagues, you're modeling that tearing down is acceptable.

You can't control your entire organization. But you can control what ripples you send into it.

Ask yourself: If everyone in my organization behaved the way I behaved, would this be a better place or a worse one?

Leading from Any Position

Leadership isn't about rank. It's about influence, and influence is available to everyone.

Formal and Informal Authority

Some people have formal authority – the rank and position that give them official power. Others have informal authority – the respect and influence they've earned through their actions. The most effective leaders have both, but informal authority is often more powerful.

You've seen this. The sergeant who has rank but no respect – whose directives are followed grudgingly and circumvented when possible. And the senior officer with no stripes who everyone looks to for guidance because they've demonstrated wisdom and integrity over years.

Building informal authority doesn't require promotion. It requires consistency – being someone others can count on, whose word means something, whose actions match their stated values.

Mentoring and Legacy

One of the most powerful forms of influence is what you pass to those who come after you. Every first responder who survives their career leaves a legacy – either of cynicism and self-protection or of wisdom and service.

If you train new personnel, formally or informally, you're shaping the next generation's experience of this profession. The question isn't whether you'll influence them – it's what influence you'll have.

Ask yourself: What do I wish someone would have told me when I started? What mistakes did I make that I could help others avoid? What wisdom have I gained that's worth passing on?

Then actually pass it on. Be available. Be honest about your struggles as well as your successes. Model the kind of first responder you wish you'd had as a mentor.

> **FIELD PERSPECTIVE**
>
> *"Twenty years in, and the thing I'm most proud of isn't any case I closed. It's the people I trained who are now training others. I can see my influence spreading – not because I was perfect, but because I was honest about what this job costs and how to pay that price sustainably."*
>
> **– Detective, 21 years of service**

When to Stay and When to Go

Not every organizational environment can be redeemed. Some are so toxic that staying damages your health regardless of what you do. The question of whether to stay or leave is one of the most consequential decisions in any first responder's career.

Reasons to Stay

Staying makes sense when:

- The toxicity is limited to certain people or areas you can avoid
- You have sufficient support systems to weather the difficulties
- You see genuine possibility for improvement – new leadership, cultural shift, policy changes

- Leaving would damage your financial security or career prospects in ways you can't absorb
- You have influence that makes things better for others

Reasons to Go

Leaving makes sense when:

- The environment is causing measurable harm to your mental or physical health
- Multiple strategies to address the toxicity have failed
- Leadership actively resists positive change
- Staying requires you to compromise your core values
- You've stayed past the point of diminishing returns

There's no universal answer. Some people need to leave environments that are destroying them. Others need to stay and be a force for change. What matters is making the decision intentionally rather than drifting into it by default.

A Note on Institutional Trauma

> If you've experienced organizational betrayal – discipline that felt unjust, being scapegoated, having your career damaged for seeking help – the wound may need professional attention.
>
> Institutional trauma is real trauma. It affects the same brain systems and produces similar symptoms to other forms of PTSI. The fact that it came from your employer rather than a call doesn't make it less significant.
>
> Many first responders need help processing organizational injuries as much as they need help processing occupational ones. If you're struggling with betrayal by your agency, consider working with a therapist who understands both trauma and organizational dynamics.

Activities for Building Professional Capital

When your organization tries to recognize or motivate you, does it usually land? If not, is the issue the *intent* or the *method*?

Have you ever raised legitimate concerns and had them dismissed as an "attitude problem"? How did that experience affect your engagement?

Does your work assignment match your wiring – providing the challenge, autonomy, and meaning you need? If not, is that something you can influence, or is it a structural mismatch?

5-Minute Quick Wins

Small actions that strengthen professional relationships.

The Genuine Acknowledgment: Today, find one colleague who did something well and tell them specifically what you noticed. Not flattery – authentic recognition. This takes one minute and builds relationship capital.

The Gossip Redirect: The next time someone starts gossiping or tearing down a colleague in your presence, change the subject or offer a different perspective. You don't have to lecture – just don't participate. Notice how it feels to break the pattern.

The Rookie Check-In: If there's someone newer than you in your organization, take five minutes to check in with them. Ask how they're doing – and listen. Remember what it was like to be new and offer what you wish someone had offered you.

The Cynicism Catch: Throughout your shift, notice when you're thinking or speaking cynically. Not skeptically – cynically. Just notice it. Awareness is the first step toward changing patterns.

15-Minute-Deep Practice

For intentional professional development.

The Organizational Stress Inventory: List the stressors in your professional life. For each one, identify whether it's occupational (inherent to the work) or organizational (a function of how your agency operates). What can you do about organizational stressors? What do you need to accept about the occupational ones?

The Professional Anchor Map: Who in your professional world genuinely supports your growth? Who would you call if you had a crisis at work? If your list is short, what could you do to build more professional anchor relationships?

The Influence Audit: Honestly assess: What influence are you having on your organization's culture? Are you making things better or contributing to toxicity? If everyone behaved the way you do, would your workplace be healthier or sicker?

The Mentoring Plan: What wisdom have you gained that's worth passing on? What mistakes could you help newer colleagues avoid? How could you make yourself more available as a mentor, formally or informally?

30-Minute Full Engagement

For comprehensive professional development.

The Organizational Betrayal Processing: If you've experienced betrayal by your organization, spend time writing about it. What happened? How did it affect you? How are you carrying it now? What would healing look like? If the wound is significant, consider this a starting point for work with a professional.

The Stay/Go Analysis: Honestly assess whether your current organization is sustainable for you long-term. What would need to change for you to thrive there? Is that change realistic? What options do you have? What would leaving cost you, and what might it give you?

The Legacy Letter: Write a letter to someone just entering this profession – not a specific person, just someone starting out. What would you want them to know? What warnings would you offer? What encouragement? This exercise clarifies what you've learned and what you want to pass on.

The Counter-Cynicism Project: Identify one way cynicism has taken hold in your organization. Develop a specific plan to counter it – not with naivety, but with healthy skepticism and action. What would it take? Who could you enlist? What's one step you could take this week?

Chapter Ten Reflection

Consider these questions honestly. Your answers are for you alone.

- What organizational stressors are affecting you most right now?
- Have you experienced organizational betrayal? How are you carrying it?
- Where do you fall on the skepticism-to-cynicism spectrum? Has it shifted over time?
- Who are your professional anchors – colleagues who genuinely support you?
- What influence are you having on your organization's culture?
- What legacy do you want to leave for those who come after you?

Chapter Eleven

The Journey Continues

You made it to the end of this book. That matters more than you might think.

In a profession that normalizes suffering and stigmatizes self-care, you chose to spend hours reading about wellness. You engaged with ideas that probably challenged you. You completed activities that required honesty about where you are and where you want to be. That's not nothing. That's the beginning of everything.

But here's what we need to be direct about: reading this book doesn't change your life. Only action changes your life. The tools in these pages work – thousands of first responders have proven that through validated research. But they only work if you use them.

> *Health is wealth.*
>
> – **Navigating Adversity Trainee**

What You Now Know

You came into this book with some understanding of wellness. Now you have a comprehensive framework – not just for surviving this profession, but for thriving in it.

You understand that your body keeps score, that unprocessed stress accumulates in physical systems that will eventually demand attention whether you give it willingly or not. You know about the endocrine system's vulnerabilities, about how shift work and chronic stress affect everything from your metabolism to your immune function.

You understand that your mindset is trainable. Psychological capital – hope, self-efficacy, resilience, optimism – isn't genetic destiny. It's a developable capacity that protects against every adversity you'll face. The research is clear: these characteristics can be built, and building them creates measurable protection.

You understand the difference between post-traumatic stress injury and disorder, between the wound and the chronic condition. You know that PTSI is a normal response to abnormal events, that it's treatable, and that the terminology matters because it shapes how we think about recovery.

You understand that emotions aren't weaknesses to be suppressed but information to be processed. You have tools for regulation – breathwork, vocabulary, transition rituals – that give you agency over your internal state rather than leaving you at its mercy.

You understand spiritual capital – the sustaining power of purpose, the three accounts that get depleted by this work, and the intentional practices that refill them. You know that burnout isn't about working too hard; it's about giving more than you're receiving without replenishing.

You understand financial capital – not just budgeting, but the wealth-building advantages of a public safety career and the dangerous behaviors that can sabotage them. You know that millionaire status is achievable on a first responder salary, and you know what gets in the way.

You understand social and professional capital – the longevity research showing that relationships are the strongest predictor of health and happiness, the value of both in-person and virtual connection, and the cultural dynamics that can either support or destroy you.

Perhaps most importantly, you now understand a distinction that most wellness programs miss entirely: not everything that looks like depression *is* depression. Not every form of exhaustion is burnout from overwork. Not every restless discomfort is anxiety.

You've learned that the four percent – people wired for high-stakes work – can experience apathy, boredom, understimulation, and person-environment mismatch in ways that mimic clinical conditions but require opposite interventions. You've learned that "rest and self-care" can worsen conditions rooted in too little meaningful challenge rather than too much demand. You've learned that being treated generically – having recognition fall flat, trust ruptures go unrepaired, and work assignments that don't match your wiring – creates its own cascade of organizational stress that traditional frameworks don't capture.

This understanding changes everything about how you approach your own wellness. Instead of applying one-size-fits-all solutions, you can now ask the diagnostic questions that reveal what you're facing – and choose interventions that address the real root cause.

You have tools. You have frameworks. You have understanding. The question now is what you'll do with them.

The Numbers That Matter

We've referenced research throughout this book. Here's what it shows for those who apply these tools:

Heroes Project Outcomes

Results from over 10,000 first responders who completed Navigating Adversity training:

- 68% improvement in overall wellness
- 36% increase in positive psychological capital
- 32% decrease in mental distress symptoms
- 26% reduction in depression
- 28% reduction in anxiety
- 34% reduction in stress

Of participants who began with severe PTSI symptoms: 100% ended with normal scores.

These aren't motivational numbers. This is what happens when people do the work.

The caveat has been repeated throughout this book because it's the most important thing we can tell you: you must do the work. Reading doesn't create change. Practice creates change. The difference between those who transformed their wellbeing and those who didn't wasn't intelligence, wasn't severity of symptoms, wasn't years of service. It was whether they applied the tools consistently.

For Those Just Starting

If you're early in your career – your first years, maybe your first decade – this message is especially for you.

You have something that veterans would give almost anything to reclaim: time. Every tool in this book becomes more powerful the earlier you apply it. The breathwork practices you establish now will be automatic by the time you face your hardest calls. The financial habits you build now will compound into security that protects your entire family. The relationships you invest in now will be the anchors that hold you steady through whatever comes.

You're also entering this profession at a moment when the conversation about wellness has finally opened. The stigma hasn't disappeared, but it's weaker than it's ever been. You have permission to take care of yourself that previous generations had to fight for – or ignore the need for, at tremendous cost.

Don't waste that advantage. Don't assume you'll deal with wellness "later" when you're more established or when things get hard. Later is too late. The patterns you establish in your first years will shape your entire career.

A Note on Your Generation

> If you're Gen Z or a younger Millennial, you've grown up hearing criticism about your generation – that you're fragile, that you can't handle adversity, that you need too much support.
>
> Here's what the research shows: you're more willing to acknowledge struggles and seek help than previous generations. That's not weakness – that's wisdom. The veterans who 'toughed it out' often did so at enormous cost to their health, their relationships, and their lives.

You're also navigating challenges previous generations didn't face: a loneliness epidemic, the dissolution of third places, social media's psychological impact, and economic uncertainty that makes financial planning harder than ever.

The tools in this book work across generations. Use them. And don't let anyone convince you that taking care of yourself is somehow less honorable than destroying yourself for the job

For Those Deep In

If you've been doing this work for years – if you're carrying accumulations of calls, of organizational betrayals, of losses that never got processed – this message is for you.

It's not too late.

The patterns you've developed can be changed. The injuries you're carrying can be healed. And some of what you've been carrying may not be what you thought it was. If you've spent years believing you were burned out, depressed, or broken – but traditional interventions never quite worked – consider that you may have been addressing the wrong condition. The four percent often get misdiagnosed because their symptoms look like the general population's but have different roots. Part of your healing journey may involve finally naming what was happening – and discovering that the "incurable" condition responds to interventions no one thought to try.

The research shows that even severe symptoms respond to intervention. People who began Navigating Adversity training with serious PTSI completed it with normal scores. That's not because their experiences were erased – it's because they developed the capacity to integrate them.

You have something newer responders don't: perspective. You know what this job costs because you've paid it. You know which coping mechanisms work and which ones just delay the reckoning. You know who you can trust and who's performing. That knowledge, combined with the tools in this book, positions you not just to heal yourself but to influence the culture for those coming behind you.

Your legacy isn't just what you did on calls. It's what you leave in people. The rookies you train, the colleagues you support, the culture you help create – that's what persists after you're gone. Healing yourself puts you in position to heal others.

The Path Forward

So, what now? You've finished the book. What do you do tomorrow?

Start Small

Don't try to revolutionize everything at once. That's a recipe for overwhelm and abandonment. Instead, pick one thing from each chapter that resonated and commit to practicing it for the next month.

Maybe it's the physiological sigh when you feel stress rising. Maybe it's the win log at the end of each shift. Maybe it's the transition ritual between work and home. Maybe it's tracking your spending for the first time. Pick practices that feel achievable and build from there.

Find Your People

Wellness in isolation is possible but harder. Finding even one person to share this journey with – a colleague working through the same material, a partner willing to support your practices, a mentor who's further along the path – dramatically increases your likelihood of sustained change.

This doesn't have to be formal. It can be a text thread where you share what you're practicing. It can be a monthly conversation about how things are going. It can be virtual if that's what works for your schedule. The point is connection and accountability.

Return to This Material

This book isn't meant to be read once and shelved. The concepts land differently depending on where you are in your career and life. Trainees who return to Navigating Adversity after a year consistently report discovering things they missed the first time – not because the material changed, but because they did.

Keep this book accessible. When you're facing a specific challenge, return to the relevant chapter. When you feel yourself slipping into old patterns, revisit the tools. When someone you care about is struggling, share what helped you.

Get Help When Needed

Nothing in this book replaces professional support when professional support is needed. If you're struggling with symptoms that aren't responding to self-help, if you're having thoughts of suicide, if your functioning is significantly impaired – please reach out to someone qualified to help.

Crisis Resources

988 Suicide & Crisis Lifeline – Call or text 988

Safe Call Now – 1-206-459-3020 (24/7, first responder specific)

First Responders Children's Foundation

Copline – 1-800-267-5463

Fire/EMS Helpline – 1-888-731-3473

Your department's EAP, peer support program, or chaplain

Asking for help isn't weakness. It's the same thing you'd tell a citizen in crisis. The rules don't change because you wear a uniform.

Voices from the Journey

We want to close with the words of first responders who've traveled this path before you. Their experiences shaped this book, and their voices remind us why this work matters.

"I completed the training! To me, there was not a single boring moment throughout the entire program. I am thankful for the precious knowledge learned and practical skill sets offered. I called it my 'soul food.'"

"I'm glad to say that I used a lot of topics covered in the course to overcome a difficult time in my personal life. Loss of my younger brother from a sudden heart attack, then a week later my mother. Then I spent 40 days in the hospital with COVID, 20 in the ICU. But I used what I learned in this course to overcome – to truly understand what resilience means. Now I know I have it."

"Public safety is not an easy job. I think you prepare for the worst physical injury, but no one discusses the emotional effect. Yes, in the academy they glaze over emotional health, but it is not a norm in our culture. Courses like this help change that culture and help individuals identify what works for them."

"A first responder doesn't need to be always like a rock. Undercurrents, feelings, especially emotions are often suppressed. It's okay and healthy to be vulnerable and to seek help when needed."

"Very well thought out course. Most, if not all, that was presented has an influence on my everyday life. I just wish a program like this was available when I started 25 years ago."

– Law Enforcement Veteran

"One of the best parts of Navigating Adversity is the reminder that we're not alone. We all serve the public in different ways and are impacted by what we see. None of us leaves this profession unscathed. Dare I suggest that this book is therapy masked as training? Call it what you will. It is equally challenging and rewarding...if you want it to be."

"Navigating Adversity reaffirms what you are doing well and gives strategies on how to improve in other areas. There's something in here for everyone."

A Final Word

You chose a profession that most people can't handle. You run toward what others run from. You carry burdens that civilians can't imagine. You've seen things that stay with you and done things that haunt you and sacrificed in ways that no paycheck can compensate.

That sacrifice deserves to be honored – not just by the communities you serve, but by you. You deserve to be healthy. You deserve to have relationships that sustain you. You deserve financial security. You deserve purpose that doesn't cost you everything else. You deserve to finish this career and live well after it.

The tools exist. The research validates them. The path is marked by those who've walked it before you. And now you know something most wellness programs don't teach: that who you are – your wiring, your needs, your uniqueness – determines which tools will work for you. One-size-fits-all solutions are for the 96%. You deserve interventions designed for who you are.

Now it's your turn.

> *There is no resilience without adversity. And you – you were built for both.*

Your 30-Day Commitment

Before you close this book, make it concrete. What will you do?

- ONE physical practice I'll commit to for the next 30 days:
- ONE psychological capital practice I'll commit to for the next 30 days:
- ONE relationship I'll invest in over the next 30 days:
- ONE financial action I'll take in the next 30 days:
- ONE person I'll share this material with:
- ONE question I'll ask myself when I'm struggling (Am I depleted from too much demand, or understimulated from too little meaningful challenge?):
- When I'll revisit this book (specific date):

Stay Connected

To learn more about Navigating Adversity training programs, resources, and community:

www.pathfinderresilience.com

The journey continues – and you don't have to walk it alone.

References

1. Mitchell, C. L. (2017). Preemployment psychological screening of police officer applicants: Basic considerations and recent advances. In C. L. Mitchell & E. H. Dorian (Eds.), Advances in psychology, mental health, and behavioral studies (APMHBS). Police psychology and its growing impact on modern law enforcement (p. 28–50).

2. Chapman, G. D. (2010). The Five Love Languages. Farmington Hills, MI: Walker Large Print.

3. van der Kolk, B. (2014). The Body Keeps the Score: Brain, Mind, and Body in the Healing of Trauma. Viking Press.

4. National Institute of Mental Health (2024). Post-Traumatic Stress Disorder. https://www.nimh.nih.gov/health/topics/post-traumatic-stress-disorder-ptsd

5. Osinga, F. (2006). Science, Strategy and War: The Strategic Theory of John Boyd. London: Taylor & Francis.

6. Swart, T. (2019). The Source: The Secrets of the Universe, the Science of the Brain. San Francisco: Harper Collins.

7. Friedman, C. (2005). Spiritual Survival for Law Enforcement. St. Petersburg, FL: Compass Publishing.

8. Myers, I. B. (1962). The Myers-Briggs Type Indicator: Manual. Consulting Psychologists Press.

9. Keirsey, D., & Bates, M. M. (1984). Please understand me: Character & temperament types. 5th ed. Del Mar, CA: Gnosology Books.

10. Carleton, R.N., et al. (2020). Assessing the Relative Impact of Diverse Stressors among Public Safety Personnel. International Journal of Environmental Research and Public Health, 17, 1234.

11. Bandura, A. (2004). Health Promotion by Social Cognitive Means. Health Education & Behavior, 31(2), 143–164.

12. Stajkovic, A. D., & Luthans, F. (2003). Behavioral management and task performance in organizations: Conceptual background, meta-analysis, and test of alternative models. Personnel Psychology, 56(1), 155–194.

13. Seligman, M.E.P. (1998). Learned Optimism. New York: Pocket Books (Simon and Schuster).

14. Rutter, M. (2006). Implications of Resilience Concepts for Scientific Understanding. Annals of the New York Academy of Sciences, 1094(1), 1-12.

15. Huberman, A. (2021). The Science of Emotions & Relationships. Huberman Lab Podcast.

16. Waldinger, R. & Schulz, M. (2023). The Good Life: Lessons from the World's Longest Scientific Study of Happiness. Simon & Schuster.

17. Holt-Lunstad, J., Smith, T.B., & Layton, J.B. (2010). Social Relationships and Mortality Risk: A Meta-analytic Review. PLoS Medicine, 7(7).

18. Luthans, F., Youssef, C.M., & Avolio, B.J. (2007). Psychological Capital: Developing the Human Competitive Edge. Oxford University Press.